How to Believe in Love Again

in Love Again

Opening to Forgiveness, Trust, and Your Own Inner Wisdom

Laura Lee Carter

MA, Transpersonal Counseling Psychology

MIMBRES PUBLISHING • Silver City, NM

How to Believe in Love Again: Opening to
Forgiveness, Trust, and Your Own Inner Wisdom

Cover design by Ann Harbour (www.ahtechservices.com)
Interior design and page composition by Sarah Johnson

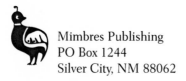

Mimbres Publishing
PO Box 1244
Silver City, NM 88062

ISBN: 0-9658404-6-8

This one is for Mike—

If I know what love is,
it is because of you.
~Herman Hesse

Abundance is how we live in each moment—
the choice to be open, the choice to entertain
the possibility that we can have, create,
and attract what we truly want.

Contents

How to Believe in Love Again

Opening to Forgiveness, Trust, and Your Own Inner Wisdom

Introduction

> So many of our dreams at first seem impossible,
> then they seem improbable, and then when we
> summon the will, they soon become inevitable.
>
> ~Christopher Reeve

Most of us start out believing that love can transform our lonely existence into something better. When that doesn't work out as hoped for or planned, do we dare dream again?

I say YES!

As the years go by, most of us slowly realize that love is what matters most. Love is what we all seek. The experience of love is vital to healing and wholeness. In a world filled with sadness, misunderstandings, and unfairness, love is our chance to feel a little less alone. No one can buy that marvelous feeling of unconditional acceptance, loyalty, and caring. Rich or poor, we have to find it for ourselves.

Many go in search of romantic love with one gigantic, unacknowledged obstacle standing in their way: difficult memories of past loves that went horribly wrong. Most of us know all too well that love can be cruel. How do you get past early disillusioning experiences that stand solidly in your path to ever believing in love again? How do you get to the point where you can fully acknowledge past negative or destructive relationships, thank them for all they have taught you, and then feel certain you have removed their power over your future? How can you find the courage to open to love again, when your mind is filled with memories of a painful past?

These are the questions I hope to answer for those who have lost their way but would still like to believe in love again.

For if we do not believe love can happen and can be so much more wonderful than ever before, there is no point to going in search of it. You must find the faith inside that love can transform your life, before it can ever happen.

My mind goes back to 1979. I was 24, and my life felt excruciatingly painful. I saw no reason to go on. A man I was hopelessly in love with had summarily dumped me for a friend I had recently introduced him to, and I had also just lost a job I really needed. Nothing made sense.

My roommate's mother came to visit us. She seemed old and very wise to me, so I found a quiet moment to ask her when life would finally settle down and make sense again. To this day, I remember her simple reply: *"Life will get better, but it's going to take quite a while."*

Those were not the words I wanted to hear, but she was exactly right.

Unfortunately, we all have to be young sometime. We all have so much to learn about ourselves and how the world works. There is no way to fast-forward and suddenly find we have the wisdom of our elders. We have to learn more each day until we begin to get how things work. It is only then that we may finally have the confidence and tools to create the lives we choose. We are all on schedule.

In the meantime, give yourself a break. Give yourself love and compassion for fighting the good fight.

No one was ever wise by chance.   ~Seneca

Why I wrote this book

Since the house is on fire, let us warm ourselves.

~Italian proverb

When I lost my career as a librarian in early 2004, I was 49 and divorced with no kids. Lucky me, I was given five months' warning that my life was about to change dramatically. The career I had counted on for decades for my bread and butter was about to disappear before my very eyes.

I became totally focused on "What's next?" The rational, practical, librarian side of my brain told me to go get another job doing exactly what I had always done. But since there were no openings in librarianship, and for years I had been dying to try something completely different, I decided to go way out on a limb and try an experiment. I slowly gathered together enough courage to follow my heart this time and switch to plan B.

Plan B was what I really wanted to do. It was my heart's desire to open my own version of a non-Internet-based match-making service. I figured, "Why not?" I certainly needed a date and a job! I had a graduate degree in counseling psychology; why not use that background and experience to change my life while helping others find love?

I also felt personally frustrated with the current dating scene. I didn't see how I was ever going to find love again, especially if my only option was through the Internet. I figured there must be millions who felt exactly the way I did, all looking for a safer, more personal alternative.

Little did I know that my new business venture would nudge me towards an illuminating personal journey, the search for a new belief in love. At that time I was unaware that my deeper purpose was to find a way to get unstuck from my decades-old negative beliefs about love. It seems my inner wisdom was determined to guide me towards a rejuvenated approach to love and life.

Luckily, the love goddesses were smiling! My friends and I had a hilarious time thinking up some "not ready for prime-time" names for my new service, names like Desperate Daters, Horny Toad Dating Service, Cynical Singles, Relationship Retards, or the Do U Believe Singles Club. After much laughter and kidding, I settled on *Intriguing Possibilities* and opened for business in the spring of 2004.

In contrast to online dating, my own approach was completely personal. I met with all new clients, both men and women, individually for an hour or two to fully grasp their history with love and then to find out what they were looking for next. Of course I performed background checks, set up an exclusive database, and then started providing get-togethers for members to meet and mix.

By owning my own dating service, I quickly learned the first major problem with these kinds of pursuits. They focus all of their energy on finding you the right date rather than helping you find a more positive perspective on love in general. With so many of us traumatized by past betrayals, or stuck mentally in what feels like permanent cynicism or defensiveness in the face of love, finding another date is not the answer. I quickly learned how many of us see love as an unrealistic illusion. I also discovered the folly of going through the motions of searching for romantic love when you feel so wounded inside from past disappointments.

Through interviews with hundreds of midlife singles, I found that most of us have a backstory that strongly impacts how we see ourselves and what we think we deserve when it comes to love. You know, those bad experiences from decades ago, when you felt so ashamed and rejected and you knew that love was not for you. Perhaps it was some extremely painful experience with unrequited love that convinced you to never give your heart again. Deep down in your unconscious, lurking quietly, there may be persistent and unfriendly voices that repeat over and over to never, ever trust another again with your heart. Sometimes it feels like a permanent certainty that you do not deserve to meet someone who has the potential to love you unconditionally. Or perhaps you feel like you have done everything you can to improve yourself, but everyone else seems damaged beyond repair.

It is essential that each of us revisit our abandonment or betrayal stories, and especially the lessons we think we have learned from them. How has your perception of that story changed over the years? How about the deep and abiding shame you may feel from previous breakups? Has your self-concept changed since then? Do you need a reality check? Does that old rejection hold far more power than it should in your present world?

Recent brain research shows that we remember most clearly those things we experienced while we were in the midst of strong emotions. Difficult life experiences may stick with us for decades, often holding more power than they deserve, especially when they have caused severe psychic trauma. It is only through a careful reassessment of these experiences and then a little patient, careful "soul surgery" that we may regain our original belief in the power of love to improve our lives and our right to receive it.

This book is designed to help you become a private detective in service to your own self-awareness and self-development. If you wish to gather a deeper understanding of why you fear love so much, and then search out those experiences in your past that have kept you stuck in your old ways of perceiving love, this book can help. Together we will explore those negative love experiences from your past where you lost your trust of others—those bad times that now sabotage your present faith that you might ever find love again.

Only by first raising your awareness of sensitive areas around your own personal roadblocks—like shame, trust, and forgiveness—and then creating new ways to work through past emotional obstacles, is it possible to access a healthier belief in all that love might have to offer you now.

Why do we need love?

As a species, we cannot help ourselves. Dr. Helen Fisher has conducted extensive research on the evolution, expression, and chemistry of love. (Please see her many books, including *Why We Love: The Nature and Chemistry of Romantic Love.*) She has found the answers to such questions as why we choose the lovers we do and how men and women vary in their romantic feelings, and she has explored the frontiers of the human brain in love.

Dr. Fisher is now convinced that love is a foundation stone of human social life. Her research results changed her thinking about the essence of romantic love. She has come to see love as "a fundamental human drive. Like the craving for food and water and the maternal instinct, it is a physiological need, a profound urge, an instinct to court and win a particular mating partner." And when love is scorned, all sorts of bad things may follow: depression, stalking, homicide, and even, sometimes, suicide.

Evidence of romantic love is found in 90% of human cultures worldwide. To quote Dr. Fisher, "Being in love is universal to humanity; it is a part of human nature, and the capacity for romantic love is woven firmly into the fabric of the human brain."

What do you believe about love now?

Learn to pretend there's more than love that matters.

~Indigo Girls

We all have to start somewhere in our journey back to believing in love again. No matter how we have been betrayed in our past, most of us started out certain that love would improve our lives. In fact, when we were young, love seemed like the answer to all our problems. Unfortunately, later in life it may seem like the cause!

Let's see what you now believe about love. Put an X next to all statements that describe your feelings most of the time:

____ Finding an appropriate love partner is now a high priority for me.

____ Sharing love is the most meaningful experience in life.

____ I believe I am worthy of unconditional love and compassion.

____ I love and accept myself exactly the way I am.

____ I have a circle of family and friends who love and appreciate me exactly the way I am.

____ I let go of relationships if they make me feel used or if they drag me down or damage me.

____ I clear up misunderstandings with others as soon as they occur.

____ I feel loving others teaches me much about myself.

____ Feeling loved and appreciated makes me feel good about myself.

_____ A loving relationship is a safe and healthy place to get my needs met.

_____ I believe we are all loveable in some way.

_____ I believe I deserve to be loved for exactly who I am.

_____ I believe I have the right to ask for what I want and need in relationships.

_____ I say no to anyone at any time if I feel taken advantage of or abused.

_____ I accept that some people will not like me. I can bear their lack of approval.

_____ A relationship means that my partner will listen to and honor what I have to say.

_____ I quickly sense when I am around toxic people and leave immediately.

_____ Being in love renews my energy, making me feel like I can do anything.

_____ I believe I will find the kind of love I seek if I approach it with an open heart.

_____ I believe there are many others just like me, seeking the love they need.

Where do you stand on the love quiz? Were you able to answer yes to most of these questions? Self-love and acceptance is the first step towards believing in love again. If we cannot find a way to love ourselves unconditionally, how will we ever learn to accept others in that way?

Why is it so hard to believe in love these days?

Life shrinks or expands in proportion to one's courage.   ~Anais Nin

As the previous owner of a dating service and as a life-change coach, I have been asked many things, but fundamentally my clients' queries come down to these two:

"Do you believe people can really change?" and "How do I begin to believe in love again?"

My clients may feel like they are ready to meet Mr. or Ms. Right, but underneath all that certainty, underneath the bluster and facade, is a deep yearning to believe that love is available to them again. It is my job to convince them that we are all constantly in the process of changing ourselves and our lives, and we are all utterly and completely loveable. I have found that love can happen to anyone at any time, and often even better as we age. But it does not just happen by chance. Working on the way you see and treat yourself and everyone else in your life improves your chances of finding love again.

It is not surprising that we struggle to have faith in love. Especially as we age, we may become convinced that romantic love is no longer possible. We are constantly bombarded with negative messages. Our very culture has become cynical in the face of love. The media constantly reminds us how prevalent divorce is, focusing on the hateful attitudes of so many nasty breakups. Conflict sells, and if it bleeds it leads. When was the last time you saw a news story focused on the importance of finding love or the beauty of finding love later in life?

But that is exactly what we need more of, not another story about a hateful divorce. We need to surround ourselves with examples of how love later in life can be so much better than those early, insecure attempts at making someone else love us.

With increasing levels of self-respect and self-acceptance most of us naturally become better at giving and receiving love. As we mature—especially if divorce or the death of a spouse has given us time to ourselves—we are better able to focus on life lessons learned. We have had time to develop into our true selves, the people we were meant to be all along. And if we are lucky, we may finally trust that if we allow ourselves to become exactly who we are, someone will come along and find us utterly loveable exactly the way we are. Increased self-respect and self-acceptance lead inevitably to a fuller acceptance of others, in all of our shared human imperfection.

So if we are all agreed that we now want and need love in our lives, how do we access it in a way that does not destroy us in the process? How do we begin to believe in romantic love as a positive force in our lives all over again?

How did we lose our ability to trust others?

The day a child realizes that all adults are imperfect
he becomes an adolescent; the day he forgives
them, he becomes an adult; the day he forgives
himself, he becomes wise.   ~Aiden Nowlan

Babies are born to be love sponges. We are all born completely helpless and in need of constant love and attention to survive. Babies have no sense of good or evil, they only know that they crave the feeling of being loved and valued. And if we were extremely lucky, our families surrounded us with the powerful feeling of unconditional love. While growing up, we were fully appreciated for our unique and special qualities without having to earn our parents' love or struggle for any form of positive attention.

Children are born with no self-concept. They are pure sensation and potential. They have no separate sense of self. They decide who they are by looking into their parents' faces. From this feedback they unconsciously decide how they feel about themselves, whether they are loveable, acceptable, talented, capable, or even worth being around. It is impossible to give too much love to a child. Children need love, acceptance, and attachment the way they need calcium to grow up straight and tall.

Unfortunately, most of us did not have this experience in childhood. A more common scenario is that of parents manipulating us with access to love. "If you act like this, then we'll love you." In other words, love became a commodity to be earned with good behavior.

Children intuitively move from discomfort to comfort, and one of the most traumatic discomforts for a child is the sudden withdrawal of a parent's love and approval. For small children, love deprivation is psychic trauma that causes them to lose their natural sense of fearlessness and spontaneity. Children will do anything to conform to parents' wishes so as not to suffer future love deprivation. Withdrawing love can work very well in disciplining kids, but it also can cause deep psychological scars. Children learn that love is conditional. They are indirectly given the message that they are not loved in and of themselves but that they must do as they are told to be worthwhile.

Along with the awareness that we must learn how to earn love and acceptance came our first experiences with feelings of betrayal and abandonment. For a small child, the threat of losing the love and support of your parents is paramount. Fears about them losing you or leaving you somewhere reflected your deepest anxieties, because you knew on a deeper level that you could not survive without them. Even as a small child, you may have unconsciously developed strategies to "make yourself useful" in an effort to ensure your own emotional survival. Parental love and concern were essential to survival, and you felt that in every bone in your body.

Shame versus guilt

The loss of trust in childhood is usually intimately intertwined with early experiences of shame. Historically, psychoanalytic psychologists focused much more on the power of guilt in creating emotional discomfort in the parent-child relationship. Recent research has found that shame plays a central role in most of the major emotional disorders of our times. Helen

Block Lewis, a pioneer in shame research, felt that the simplest and most clear distinction between guilt and shame is that shame is usually felt towards the self, while guilt is more often embarrassment about our actions towards others.

Perhaps the best way to distinguish these two parallel emotions is to compare their primary affects. When people feel ashamed, they usually feel inadequate, deficient, worthless, exposed, or disgraced. In contrast, guilty people might feel bad, evil, wicked, remorseful, or responsible for actions towards others. Shame can also elicit a sense of not belonging, abandonment, or a lost sense of self. Primary to the experience of shame is a lack of trust towards others.

From the fundamental discomfort of low self-esteem and poor self-concept to the severest cases of depression, violence against others, eating disorders, addictions, and dissociative disorders, shame has been found to play a key role. In the past few decades, many tradition-bound psychoanalytic practitioners have turned away from Freud's theories on unconscious guilt and turned towards shame as a pervasive and yet seriously neglected and misunderstood emotion in contemporary society.

Shame and trust issues

According to shame theorists, feelings of shame can be most disturbing to a child's development of a sense of self and personal identity. Gershen Kaufman, a clinical psychologist well known for his research in shame theory, feels that in the context of normal development, shame is often the primary source of low self-esteem, diminished self-image, poor self-concept, and deficient body image. Shame can also produce a lack of confidence and security, which may create a long-term and pervasive impediment to the experience of trust, belonging, or shared intimacy. Other common problems, such as feelings of alienation, loneliness, inferiority, and perfectionism, have been directly linked to early severe shaming. Kaufman's list of "shame-based syndromes" includes physical abuse, sexual abuse, addictions, and eating disorders. Shame also plays a central role in pathological disorders such as clinical depression, paranoia, and borderline personality.

Much theory has arisen out of wondering how a person develops a sense of shame around certain emotions or experiences. Both our physiological drives, such as hunger and sexuality, and our primary interpersonal drives can be bound with shame at an early age. This means that as a child experiences basic needs like the need for love or attention, those desires become correlated either with pleasure or with negative affects like shame and disgust. With the child's first experience with each need, emotions may attach to these experiences, which may then become bound with shame, so that when that emotion is felt later (for example, dependency on others, fear, or powerlessness) the child only feels full of shame.

Parental anger is often the child's first experience with difficult or debilitating shame. This experience can create a rupture in the vital emotional link between parent and child, and the shame can feel to the child like, "You don't like me anymore." While anger can be unavoidable, the parent-child interpersonal link needs be restored later, through touching and holding the preverbal child or verbal reassurance of the older child. Failure to restore this link can intensify the rupture, leaving the child trapped in a feeling of intense shame.

Early shaming experiences, particularly when repeated or prolonged over time, can escalate into severe fears of abandonment. Shame is often consciously used as a method of control with older children. The earlier and the more often children are shamed, the more pliant they become to unfair and abusive treatment from their caretakers. These shaming experiences feel threatening to children's very survival at a point in self-development when they are not capable of an accurate assessment of reality.

What is usually unconscious in these interactions is the intergenerational nature of this strategy of control and manipulation. Shaming patterns can be deeply rooted in the parents' own childhood experiences and can reemerge and be reactivated in the process of child rearing. Thus the shame-based family system is perpetuated. Some of the different ways parental shaming can be communicated to the child are: "Shame on you!", "You are so embarrassing to me!", "I'm so disappointed in you," or any sort of belittling disparagements, including names like stupid, clumsy, fatso, or sissy. Unfortunately, shaming is often minimized as simply a form of humor or teasing. Many families are organized around such pervasive teasing, which then becomes a potent source of shame.

Childhood   There are a number of contradictory theories on how shame is originally experienced and how early in life shame can be felt. Even a mother's emotional state during pregnancy may have an impact on the unborn child's emotions. New research shows that a mother's mental state long before giving birth can have an effect on the temperament and personality of her child. (See Annie Murphy Paul's *Origins: How the Nine Months Before Birth Shape the Rest of Our Lives*.) If the mother feels depressed, anxious, or unhappy about her pregnancy, the fetus picks up these emotions. In addition, after birth but before the child is able to communicate successfully with others, shameful emotions may be felt. Research has shown that children do sometimes suffer preverbal emotional abuse and trauma long before they have the words to describe their experiences.

Shaming experiences at an early age can be profoundly destructive to a child's sense of self-worth, trust, and future ability to bond with others. A sense of trust needs to be established early in a child's life for healthy relationship skills to develop. The earliest and most basic aim of social behavior is the striving for intimate relations with a caring other person.

Shame results from a crisis in trust between parent and child. The mother and father serve as representations of how others will respond to the child. A child needs to be looked at, smiled at, and approved of by an active, loving, and supportive person. Poor mirroring by the primary caretaker can cause feelings of inadequacy and shame in the child, feelings that can remanifest in adolescence and adulthood when the person is faced with unusual amounts of trauma or stress like a serious illness, unemployment, or the breakup of an important, meaningful relationship.

Adolescence   Let's face it, most of us were somehow scarred by adolescence. According to Gershen Kaufman, the hormonal and physical changes brought on by puberty make adolescence "a developmental epoch during which there is a rapid magnification of shame." Changes in the voice; facial blemishes; and body hair, breast, and genital development all call attention to the self, causing increased feelings of self-consciousness, shyness, and fear of unfriendly attention from others. The primary feeling attached to adolescence is shame—shame around being exposed and scrutinized by others; shame around intimacy and sexuality; shame for males around expressing affection, tenderness, touching (especially other males), or crying publicly; shame for females around expressing anger or asserting power.

The three "central cultural scripts" of our society come strongly into play in adolescence. These are the issues Kaufman sees as the primary shame activators specific to our culture: competition for success, independence/self-sufficiency, and the need to be popular and conform.

At the same time, we are bombarded with messages from the media and our friends to go in search of romantic love. Finding an appropriate lover raises social status and proves that at least one person in this world finds you irresistible. Very early on we learn the importance of finding and keeping romantic love.

But in junior high and high school it seems that only the cool kids have access to romantic love. They appear to have so much more confidence in themselves and love seems to come naturally to them. But if you happen to be one of the "cool kids," it probably doesn't feel that way. With puberty and sexual experimentation, the confusion continues. "How do I distinguish between love and sexual desire? Why don't they teach classes in this? Are we just supposed to know what to do when we fall in love the first time?"

Nobody knew back when we were adolescents that our frontal-lobe development wouldn't be complete until our mid-twenties. Since our frontal lobe controls insight, judgment, and impulse control, we were free to make all the stupid mistakes of youth, and we did.

Many early "love" relationships that begin in high school and college are, for the most part, total disasters, marked by constant breakups and then that glorious feeling of making up. This is the time when we play at love, testing out our egos and power over others. It is not uncommon for our earliest relationships to include much shaming and blaming, as well as some emotional, if not physical, abuse. We generally have no idea what we are doing, and with little impulse control or understanding of what we are experiencing, cruelty is common and mistakes are made.

Only by entering into more mature, loving relationships much later do we realize the low quality of our earliest attempts at bonding with others. But even then, it can be difficult to end the destructive cycle created by early shaming experiences, which lead to future dysfunctional relationship patterns. Love has come to be defined as a challenging, shameful, painful struggle. First loves may be painful or even abusive, and that is how we come to define relationships. That becomes the familiar pattern, so much so that it may feel strange and even suspicious when love is given freely with no apparent strings attached.

Adulthood Shame researcher Kaufman defined four general classes of shame activators for adulthood in our culture. Vocation, feelings of powerlessness, relationships, and aging are the experiences that are most commonly tied to shame as we mature. Because we all experienced a primitive sense of helplessness and powerlessness at birth and as small children, we are conditioned to seek power over our lives as we age. Maturation gradually shrinks feelings of powerlessness and strengthens our perception of inner control. But anytime we experience a life event that wrenches away this sense of inner control, for example, the breakup of an important relationship, we are naturally brought back to negative emotions connected with earlier primitive feelings of powerlessness, fear, anger, distress, defeat, failure, and loss. This process can spontaneously reactivate primary shame issues in our lives.

Severe shaming in adulthood can cause an immediate and unconscious regression without warning, which throws us back into negative feelings experienced as children, feelings such as deep fears of abandonment, powerlessness, inadequacy, incompetence, helplessness, worthlessness, and failure. Severe public shaming can even cause dissociation, totally debilitating a normal adult with a relatively healthy ego.

Early issues with trust and dependency make it impossible for shame-based adults to conceive of being part of a relationship or even to conceive of interactions characterized by mutual respect, compassion, and decency. Often these trust issues can be traced back to childhood experiences where the child was so cruelly shamed by a trusted adult that the specific experience is generalized out to include everyone. You may feel so ashamed of yourself that you decide never to trust others and never depend on them again, because you feel no one is truly trustworthy. This is especially true in cases of emotional, physical, and sexual abuse.

Because of serious childhood shame issues, your first major betrayal or the breakup of an important romantic relationship may cause unconscious emotional regression to your childhood, a time when you did not have control over your environment. Because this can be such a powerfully negative experience, it may color your view of love for the rest of your life. Your early memories of feeling so abandoned and betrayed by the same person who had helped to create those first euphoric feelings of genuine human connectedness may cause you to shut down emotionally. You may deny your powerful need for the love of others for many years to come.

Early love trauma

Good judgment comes from experience, and a lot of
that comes from bad judgment.   ~Barry LePatner

The loss of early love: A case study

That room, like a box of pain.   ~Marge Piercy

I wake up every morning alone and crying. It takes me just a
moment to remember the disaster my life has become since
you left me. I thought we were in love. I thought you were
truly there for me. How could you suddenly decide to take off
with my friend?

Feelings of utter devastation return. I placed all of my trust
in you. I thought we were a couple. I thought you loved me,
and I trusted my friend too. I cannot believe you two can now
be so cruel to me. It's like you have turned into a different
person, one I never saw when we first met. And when I confront you, you add insult to injury by saying, "This sort of thing
happens all the time." This may happen all the time, but not
to me!

I feel speechless with sadness and anger, both at the same
time. Who is this mean, hateful person you have become? I
wish I could understand why you have changed so completely.
Your betrayal of my love and trust has destroyed me. It feels
like I finally let someone in. I opened up and trusted you completely, letting you know the real me, and then you casually
reject everything that I am.

I guess you didn't realize how much power you had over
me, because you now shirk any responsibility for my pain. This
is the most traumatic experience of my life! How can I ever
trust men—or women—again?

"I give up on love!"

While in our teens or twenties, the trauma of being rejected by a trusted lover feels like a threat to our very existence. And because we are young and sensitive, it may convince us that deep, meaningful love never lasts. Worse than that, it may create the illusion that we have personally ruined the best relationship we have ever had. We may feel responsible even though we cannot see what we have done to bring such pain into our lives.

This kind of rejection feels utterly unfair and irrevocable, like a mistake that can never be fixed. In our young and inexperienced hearts and minds, we may see this harsh, devastating lesson as a sign that we are fundamentally unloveable and decide we are finished with love for good. These excruciating memories may be etched on our very souls. The pain can be continuous and unbearable for years to come. Like children we may decide, "I give up on love!"

The trauma may be worsened by the fact that this new emotional injury has brought up deep, unconscious childhood shame and trust issues, childhood anxieties concerning fear of rejection and abandonment, wounds that were never previously recognized or dealt with. Trauma may lie dormant for decades until a fresh emotional injury brings up deep and fundamental fears about losing the love and support we needed for survival.

Insults and injuries accumulate in a child's unconscious mind, creating shame, guilt, and anger over past experiences. Sometimes these feelings lie dormant for years, emerging suddenly in full force when a traumatic event occurs, like a major breakup in high school or college. And because the teenage and early-twenties brain has not fully developed, the ability to show proper judgment, insight, and impulse control is diminished.

We do what we can to survive this insult to our sense of self, but malignant feelings of guilt, anger, and self-loathing remain, buried deep inside. We may learn to cope, pretending to care about ourselves and others. We may even ultimately get into other relationships, but deep inside we know that love cannot be trusted. True love comes to mean only one thing: endless pain. It may seem childish and silly to even think about, so we may become cynical in the face of love, deciding only fools believe in such idealistic nonsense.

What happens when you try to ignore or simply "get over" those early betrayals? They do go away, but not very far. If you try to deny or ignore feelings of being fundamentally un-loveable, they will continue to haunt you, popping up at all the wrong times and places. Every time you see a chance at finding love again, shame and self-doubt will sabotage your efforts and make you run away. If you decide to marry, you will probably choose a partner with similar emotional wounds, because neither of you feels worthy of deep human connection and compassion. There's a very good chance that over and over again you will settle for less than you deserve. Deep down inside you know that you are unworthy of true love, so your natural tendency will be to settle for much less.

Years later, perhaps when you are going through a tough divorce, job loss, or some other trauma in your life, your negative feelings about yourself may come crashing down on you—at a time when you can least defend against them. This time they may emerge stronger than ever, demanding that you give them proper attention.

Because you did not have the internal strength or the tools you needed to fully deal with bad feelings about yourself and love in your earlier years, their truth may be etched on your soul like an undeniable mantra. You may be plagued with questions like "Why can't I do relationships?" or "Why do I always choose partners who are bad for me? Why did I stay when I felt so criticized and abused? Will I ever get this right?"

The most common mistake you will make as you attempt to get past early traumas is expecting others to fix you or to know the answers to your unique quest. Rather than put in the years it may take to grieve your past with the support of an empathic, supportive coach or counselor, it is common to search externally for quick fixes. You will search in vain. It can be quite disappointing to learn that others cannot answer your most difficult questions about your life and your needs. This is the ultimate do-it-yourself job, but don't worry. You are up to the task!

We attract what we are

It is not just dumb luck or chance, whom we meet in our search for love or the kinds of partners we attract to ourselves. If we have a deep mistrust of others, we attract others who feel the same. If we are out looking for meaningless sexual encounters, we can usually attract them. If we feel we don't really deserve love, we attract others who are also feeling unworthy and emotionally unavailable. If we feel love is something to be earned with our dedication and services, we will attract others who will make us earn it.

Even if we believe we are ready for a mature, loving relationship, our feelings may beg to differ. We may be able to lie to ourselves, but our unconscious, our bodies, and the subtle energy fields around us cannot. We all give off unconscious messages to others that we may not even realize or appreciate, but we are communicating all the same, and in important ways. Until we change our deepest feelings about ourselves, about love, and about what we wish to attract into our lives, we will continue to draw to ourselves the kinds of relationships that never go anywhere we want to go.

The "I don't need anyone in my life" syndrome

Up until now, one of your rules of survival has been to try to ignore your feelings. How well did that work? Over time, by trying to suppress strong feelings, you have only increased their power. Strong negative feelings go underground into your subconscious, sabotaging your physical health and then popping back up when you are least prepared to deal with them. In times of personal crisis, those dark, mean feelings you have about yourself overwhelm you exactly when you have the least strength to defend against them. After the death of a loved one, a divorce, or a long stint of unemployment, when you already feel bad about your life circumstances and about yourself, negative feelings may reemerge and leave you feeling like the ultimate loser, because for that moment in time it seems you can do nothing right.

You have let your fear of your own feelings rule your life up until now. Part of the reason you feel so alone is that you are deathly afraid of depending on others or asking for their help. Perhaps you feel you don't deserve love and respect from others. Asking for anything from anybody makes you feel vulnerable, a feeling you do your best to avoid. You instead chose to maintain the illusion of invulnerability. That is the only way you feel safe. "It's me against the entire world!"

You know how dangerous it is to need others for anything, and besides, others simply cannot be trusted. Others can never understand what you've been through. And if you tried to tell them, you might slip and start having some real feelings for yourself and them. You might scare them away with your boundless fear and insecurity. It's best to keep all needs and feelings under wraps.

Somewhere in the mix you may also have feelings (or delusions?) of superiority. The internal monologue goes something like this: "I'm smarter than everyone else, that's why I don't need them." Instead you live in your head, denying any human need, like talking to others about your feelings. Sure, depression takes over sometimes, but that's safer than expressing your endless anger. Underneath it all, you have a sneaking suspicion that you truly have no power over your life or what happens next. You feel responsible for everything even though you can see how much you don't control. One thing is for certain. You don't deserve love simply for being here. You don't deserve attention, appreciation, acceptance, or affection. Love can only be earned by providing others with something they need.

Time to join the human race: That means asking for help

Is it time to finally admit you don't have all of the answers and your past coping skills aren't working for you anymore? Although your feelings can certainly seem overwhelming, do not even try to ignore them this time. Even though it makes you feel quite vulnerable, seek out some counseling assistance now. You will need to learn how to lean on others to complete this important journey of self-discovery. Do not delay this process any further.

Perhaps you need to take a sick day or two to honestly experience your overwhelming feelings of sadness or outrage about your past. Have you ever considered learning how to meditate? Why not start keeping a journal of your feelings and thoughts? This is the time to begin to honor all that you are and feel. You can no longer ignore how you feel about yourself. Take responsibility for all that you are and all that you hope to be. Those who are too afraid to face their deepest, most authentic feelings about their past will not be able to find love in their future.

Acknowledging and accepting the whole truth about your deepest needs, while extremely painful and difficult, can also provide a gigantic feeling of relief. Perhaps there are a few others who understand your plight and can be trusted. There is no future in blaming and shaming yourself and others. Let go of all the shame and step up to full self-responsibility.

Let go of your overwhelming feelings of shame and enter the realm of self-compassion. We are all only human. None of the things that happened to you as a child were your fault. We are all eminently loveable, and we all make mistakes in trusting the wrong people. But we are also all trainable. It's time to learn a new way to live. It's no longer "me against the world"; instead, it's me allowing the world in to teach me how to love and be loved. Learning how to live from a place of vulnerability and soothing self-compassion can feel like finally coming home. Accepting your most basic human needs for love and acceptance can feel honest and quite empowering.

Are you ready to ask for help now?

If you are certain that your present attempts at finding love are not working, you are now ready to change. Could it be that you simply do not believe in love anymore? Perhaps you've tried everything you could possibly think of to try and have still only found disappointment and despair. It may be time to lay down all those tricks you have up your sleeve and admit defeat.

All of that armoring, and the facades you have carefully constructed to hide your disillusionment and pain, are really just defenses against ever finding love again. I know you have had excellent reasons to construct them. You need to protect yourself out there! After all, you have experienced a lifetime of pain and rejection. Early shaming, rejection, or betrayal by a parent or other close family member or by a romantic partner or spouse, or the loss of a parent early in life has created gigantic trust issues for you, so you have good, rational reasons to defend against any further loss. That kind of early and traumatic rejection or betrayal does not simply go away with time, but instead undermines your core beliefs about yourself and sabotages any further attempts at finally finding a healing love.

Fears of future suffering often cause us to avoid trusting others, and so true intimacy is no longer an option. As a substitute, we may instead get involved, but never get too close, in hopes that when the relationship ends (which it always does) we will have less to lose. In this way we may unconsciously repeat the behavior patterns of our past, never moving to higher levels of love and compassion for ourselves or others.

Nothing happens without personal transformation

When we allow ourselves to remain defenseless victims, decades of our lives may pass in loneliness and fear until we one day decide this status quo cannot stand. Often this can happen only when some crisis occurs, like 9/11, the death of someone close to you, a divorce, a job loss, or a serious illness.

These types of life-changing events shock us out of our comfortable complacency, causing us to realize that our old ways of seeing the world and relating to it are not working. Raw, stunning heartbreak may create the sudden, needed realization of how fragile our lives really are. Then the questions begin: "Do I want to be like this forever?" You may finally decide it's now or never. "I must change now. I must get past my past and learn how to trust others again."

Perhaps the encouragement of someone close will help you realize how desperate you are to extract yourself from your own self-imposed solitary confinement. When it feels like we have little left to lose, we may finally decide to take the risk of trusting enough to ask for the kind of help we so desperately need. It is now time to begin taking baby steps towards relearning the art of loving others, starting with your own precious self.

When we decide it is time to take our power back and change this negative pattern, there is much we can do to reverse the power of past traumatic experiences that have stood in our way for so long. The first step is accessing enough internal strength to ask for help from others who have traveled this path before you. Finding the right counselor, coach, or guide can help. Learning how to trust one other caring person is an excellent place to start. This is a slow but necessary process. Asking for help is the first essential step towards slowly building back trust in other human beings.

For many of us, the counseling relationship can build into the experience of being reparented. This is when the therapist offers the client a positive alternative to those damaging first relationships with parents or early caretakers. Through this process, the therapist builds trust and then shows the client what a healthy, positive relationship looks and feels like, modeling healthy ways of relating and loving and offering support.

It is only through healing relationships that we can return to the belief that love is in fact out there and available to us. We were all born to love. Many of us spend a lifetime trying to deny this fact, but in the end, when our lives have passed and we lie on our deathbeds, who will we want around us?

When I started my own personal journey with counseling in my mid-thirties, I absolutely hated the idea of ever depending on anyone ever again. It took years of soul-searching and then a couple of years of counseling to convince me that I truly did need others in my life.

I had resisted this concept for years because of my painful history with abandonment and betrayal. It was a powerful and memorable moment when I finally acknowledged my deep and undeniable need to depend on the "kindness of strangers." As much as I hated to admit it, I was a social animal just like everyone else. Those who do not have the skills and trust to build positive, loving relationships don't survive as long. The sooner we acknowledge that truth, the better our lives will be.

For many of us, it may take years or even decades to finally confront the fact that we've lost our belief in love and in the wonderful ways it can transform our lives. Later, perhaps after a bad breakup or divorce, we may start to question all of our internal monologues. "What do I really believe? Is love truly hopeless? Why can't I 'do' marriage? How come I can't seem to be with others emotionally? Will I never experience love again in this lifetime? Am I doomed to live alone forever?"

It may only be when these questions float to the top that we realize how shame based our first relationships were, and that the trauma caused by those early heartbreaks closed our hearts to ever truly believing in love again. This regression can be doubly difficult if we felt somehow responsible for ruining the best relationship we had ever experienced up until then. We may have lost our ability to trust others wholeheartedly, thus dooming ourselves to only superficial relationships with little real love or trust involved.

Self-forgiveness is the place to start when you feel this way. Shame, fear, guilt, and anger are the four major obstacles to ever experiencing love again. Holding on to old emotions from decades past can take a tremendous toll over a lifetime, and only increases the suffering of all involved. Holding on to old negative experiences also drains psychic energy, energy you can use now to transform your belief system and find the kind of love you deserve.

Your challenge now is to transform all of that energy—bound up in shame, guilt, fear, and anger about past betrayals—into positive changes in yourself and your present perspective. Where to begin? You need to find a way to forgive yourself and make a conscious decision to let go of anything that happened in your past, taking full ownership of any part you might have played in it. You also need to embrace the realization of how little you control in your life. Even though you may feel responsible for just about everything that happens to you, you control very little of what happens in this world, and this was especially true when you were young.

Would you want to marry you?

Whether married or single, take a moment to ask yourself this question. I often asked it myself after I lost my marriage and then my job in my late 40s. I felt set adrift in a sea of loneliness, certain I would never date again, let alone marry. After my divorce, I could discern few positive qualities in myself. That's why I consciously chose not to date for a few years. And then, after I lost my job, I felt certain nobody would want to be with me.

But no matter your present work or marital status, do you find yourself attractive? Loveable? A pleasant partner to be around? Fun to be with? Interesting? A good investment?

If your honest answer is no, then it's time to look deeper into the reasons why you wouldn't choose you for a marriage partner. Are you excited about your life and your future? What could you do to get excited again? What could you do to again find yourself loveable and your life exciting?

If you do not find yourself loveable, it can be quite challenging to believe others will. It's now time to find a deeper level of compassion for yourself, especially if you feel unworthy of love. How can you begin to love your present self fiercely, exactly as you are?

The journey back to self-love and self-acceptance

No matter how hard one searched, one could not find anyone in the universe more deserving of love than oneself. ~Buddha

Who you are, is not the problem—even though you may have heard that your whole life. This is about everything you've done right. Not about what you've done wrong.

The more you believe in yourself, the better you perform in every part of your life. Our belief systems equal our realities. Our belief systems are combinations of our ideas, thoughts, and experiences. These all combine to determine who we believe ourselves to be.

The journey back to believing in love again must begin with finding a new and much higher level of self-respect. The secret to letting go of all the hurt and betrayal you may have suffered in your past is the slow, gentle process of giving yourself heartfelt compassion for all you have endured at the hands of others.

At the time of my own separation and divorce, I spent a few years first grieving the loss of the dream. We all have inside of us some dream of what a loving, positive relationship should look and feel like. The end of any important relationship is traumatic. Even friendly divorces can be difficult. It may not even be about the end of a relationship that we found destructive and therefore needed to end. It may be about the loss of the dream of what love might have been, how it could have made our lives more bearable and more worthwhile.

A period of grief is definitely in order before we can be ready to change enough to believe in love again. After the grief we must find a way to forgive ourselves for misjudging the situation and choosing inappropriately. What have we learned about how we are in relationships? Did we trust our intuition or inner voice when we first met our last partner? Why did we not follow our intuition's sage advice? Will we listen next time? Can we accept that we are only human and so will always make mistakes? Are we fundamentally loveable in spite of this misstep? Is there still love in our future?

When I was in the process of learning how to love myself again after my divorce, I found Gloria Steinem's book *Revolution from Within* very useful. I especially enjoyed her idea of accessing your past self for a heart-to-heart talk. She suggested imagining you are looking your past self in the eyes.

How do you feel about her? What would you like to say to her now? I found Gloria's poignant words helpful when I looked back over my life and reflected on the sad, shy girl I used to be: "She's doing the best she can. She's survived—and she's trying so hard. Sometimes I wish I could go back and put my arms around her." I found these words cathartic.

Is it possible that you might fall in love with yourself all over again? Do you remember a time when you were very young and found yourself simply delightful? This was long before the world told you to quit being so full of life. Much like a new puppy, every new thought and action seemed exciting, like a first discovery, and the world was your oyster! Before the outside world stepped in to disagree, you were an amazing child with high self-esteem, ready to be loved and accepted exactly as you were.

Wouldn't it feel wonderful to reconnect with that child? Imagine if you could meet yourself when you were three or four. Would you recognize yourself? Crazy as it may seem, you can actually recapture that feeling in the midst of your present disillusionment with love. Begin by putting all of your energy into remembering how optimistic and cool you used to be, and then add on to that how amazing you have become over the past 20, 30, or 40 years.

So much has happened since then. So many psychic injuries and traumas have taught you how to defend yourself from harm, but unfortunately all of that carefully constructed armor can get in the way of finding your true self now, as an adult. How do we get back to that child and offer her or him the needed love and encouragement to come out and play?

What happened to those kids who loved themselves so much? The world happened. We had to learn all the rules and reasons why we couldn't allow our true selves to blossom at that particular time. Well, guess what? It's high time for your best self to start shining through again. In fact it's now or never.

It is so essential that you find a way to access and appreciate your true self sometime in this lifetime. For it is only by digging deep that we find fulfillment and satisfaction. Being there for everyone else in our lives is a necessary and noble goal, but now it is time for you to find out who you are, beyond all of your relationships with others. Now is the time to take full responsibility for your life, and become the person you are inside, the person you were born to be.

It takes wisdom and courage to embark on this quest, because you have no idea what you may find. You only know you must follow through, or else you will never know who you might have been. Facing your true self as an adult takes insight, courage, and stamina. It also often takes outside assistance. Don't be afraid to ask for help through this difficult transition. Consider hiring a coach or a counselor to reparent you by shining a bright light on your past experiences that may have convinced you to never trust in others. Find a counselor whom you trust intrinsically, someone who can push you through your own personal stuck places to a new belief in the positive power of trust and love. It is now time to dig through all of your old beliefs, decide what to discard, and finally admit what you truly must have before you die. It is now time to go after your fondest dreams!

Rather than allowing your parents, your employer, your spouse, your children, your church, or the advertisers and media to define you and determine your actions, spend some time learning who you are underneath all the outside influences. With time spent solely focused on yourself and your own needs, you may begin to see all the ways you've ignored your natural talents and tendencies, how you've lived for others and not taken care of yourself properly.

Trust in your inner wisdom, acknowledging that this may be a slow process. It may even make you feel uncomfortable at times, but give yourself permission to experiment and explore, taking baby steps every day. You may run into dead ends. Just don't let them stop you. Use all the tools and resources available to you, like books, local groups and programs, music, exercise, visioning, creativity, whatever keeps you on your path of self-discovery. Remember, you do not have to do this alone, so network. Enlist the help of friends, family, and colleagues who help you believe in yourself so you can now achieve your full potential.

Realize that the picture of your new life will most likely come to you in small pieces, like a puzzle. Maintain faith that each piece will take you a little closer to the future you envision for yourself.

Enjoy the adventure of getting to know your new self. So much has changed within you since you first married, had children, or chose your present career. What do you love now? What are you truly passionate about? Make use of solitude and journaling to nurture yourself, question your old beliefs, and figure out where you need to go next.

Feel free to daydream about a better future for yourself. Some of the best ideas in human history came from daydreaming, as with Newton and his apple! Find a place where you feel the most freedom to dream a better life for yourself. Whatever you do, never give in to your greatest fear, that you are a loser or a failure.

This quest is not about career choice or partner compatibility, although it influences both of these factors in our lives. It is about getting down to the basics of life. "What is my truth that I came here to share? How have I ignored my true self to the detriment of the world? What must I do before I die to feel that I've fulfilled my purpose here on earth?" This is about finally finding a powerful sense of self-love and self-respect, one that no other person can ever threaten again.

For me, this was a time of rediscovering all the positive, creative things I loved to do but had not done in ages, things like watercolors, writing poetry, walking my dogs in beautiful, natural settings, and redecorating my house in all my favorite colors. I also kept a journal where I focused on what was great about me, instead of my old pattern of complaining about what a mess I was. Listening to positive music always lifted my spirits, as well as reading great books and watching movies that made me feel good about myself.

We must all find that self-loving place inside *before* we begin to bring others into our lives. If we do not love and respect ourselves, we can easily stray into blaming and shaming others because of our own bad feelings about ourselves. I now see how a lack of self-compassion and self-respect leads to most of the dysfunctional relationships in the world.

For extra help in this journey, you might consider reading my first book, *Midlife Magic: Becoming the Person You Are Inside,* and working your way through my *Midlife Change Workbook.* If you are struggling to feel good about yourself, please check out my short e-book, *Feel Like a Loser? What to Do When You Don't Have a Clue.*

In addition, a few classics in this field are:

- *Learning to Love Yourself* by Sharon Wegscheider-Cruse
- *How to Be an Adult in Relationships* by David Richo
- *Revolution from Within: A Book of Self-Esteem* by Gloria Steinem
- *Codependent No More* by Melody Beattie

Exploring your dark side: The power of anger

Have a sense of gratitude to everything, even
difficult emotions, because of their potential to
WAKE YOU UP!   ~Pema

For most of our lives, we have been conditioned to be nice
to others. Even when we've felt annoyed or antagonized, we
have tried to hold it all in and "play nice." Granted, if everyone
plays nice, the world is an easier place to deal with. However,
sometimes we need to acknowledge our anger at all of the
unfairness we have experienced. It can sometimes feel like all
those decades of playing nice, when we really didn't feel that
way, have finally culminated in a nuclear explosion inside.

Take the time to explore your dark side. It isn't a bad thing
to finally check out that whole other side of your personality
that you never showed to anyone for fear that they wouldn't
speak to you again. Our hidden animosities come out regularly
in our dreams. We all have a dark side, and the more vehe-
mently you resist acknowledging it, the darker it becomes. It's
there and it needs to have a voice!

Most of us are either perpetually angry at everything (as in
road rage) or have gigantic, unrealistic fears around expressing our anger to those we love. It is interesting that these two
seemingly different reactions to our own anger create similar
problems in our lives: they push others away.

What are the origins of our deep distrust of expressing our
anger? Long before Victorian times, the Christian Church defined anger as one of the seven deadly sins. For many of us, religious training played a strong role in teaching us to tune out

angry feelings. We may have been told, "A nice person doesn't get mad, especially a nice girl."

Yet religious teachers like Jesus did not deny their anger. Do you recall the Bible story about the money changers in the temple? Jesus turned over their tables in disgust. These were the actions of a passionate, articulate revolutionary. His anger shocked people out of their rigid complacency, their greed and materialism, stimulating a strong response and awakening their hearts.

Just like with shame, we seem to be very confused about anger in our society today, where it comes from and what it means. I once had a young client who pushed away all of her friends and family with temper tantrums. By working with her, I helped her to see that her anger was misdirected at those who truly cared about her. She was really feeling angry at life and its inherent cruelties. She was so hurt by life that her natural, bodily reaction was to push everyone away to make certain that no one could ever hurt her again.

Only after she'd gained this insight and awareness was she able to become vulnerable enough to feel the anguish underneath the anger. Digging deep to access her true feelings of pain and frustration helped her to eventually feel compassion for herself and all she had suffered at the hands of others. This slowly changed her conditioned response to those she cared about.

We can only push away our own deepest needs for connection with others for so long. This works when we are in pure survival mode. But to flourish and grow, we must recognize the true source of our anger and fear. There is a huge reservoir of hurt feelings behind all anger. It is deeply connected to protecting ourselves and those we love.

But some of us get stuck in anger mode. This is because it feels easier and safer to be angry than to feel the depth of pain underneath. Anger is the fundamental stance of self-protection against further betrayal and harm. But it most often leads to depression and self-destruction. We need others in our lives. We need love and support to become our best selves. We need to become vulnerable and soft at times, thus allowing ourselves to change, rather than angrily protect ourselves against others.

The power of anger is the power to restore our sense of self-worth. It says, "I am worth protecting." Always below anger are other, deeper emotions that need to be acknowledged. Deeper are the hurt, the disappointment, the vulnerability, the fear of loss, the longing for connection. Most of us resist these feelings. We find anger to be a safe place to protect our frightened selves.

If you have made the decision to learn how to believe in love again, you must first find the courage to emerge from your defensive stance and acknowledge your deeper need for human connectedness. Believing in love again may feel extremely dangerous. Human relationships are just plain demanding, and it often seems easier to simply run away. But running away only works for so long. Be honest with yourself and what you need now, even if it feels terrifying. You may find that your anger is no longer productive in getting you where you want to go in life.

Depression and anger

Underneath most sadness or depression is a seemingly inexhaustible fountain of rage stored up from decades of stuffing most of our feelings. For women this usually comes from very early training, which taught us that being angry is not ladylike. Nice girls don't feel rage and certainly don't show it. Depression and self-blame are much more acceptable in our society, especially for women.

For men the same is true, but it is definitely more acceptable for men to show righteous indignation than for women. When men get angry in our society, it is often seen as justified. When women get angry they are often judged as "bitchy."

Most of us become extremely uncomfortable when we feel like our life situation requires some strong show of anger. We fear that if we release any of our righteous indignation at the unfairness of our lives, we may explode and all of our rage will come roaring out to consume us and everyone around us.

When I was in training to learn how to release my anger in a healthy and controlled way, if I found myself feeling the need to defend myself I would sometimes start to hyperventilate at the very thought of really getting angry. I had an irrational fear of expressing rage, which came from early training that any show of anger would be punished.

Even though most of us don't have a very positive view of anger, it is actually our best measure of when or whether we are being abused. Anger comes straight from our own body wisdom and warns us that the situation we face is contentious or perhaps unfair, and we need to react in order to protect ourselves.

Deciding how much anger is required and mediating its release is a method we must learn from carefully studying our own history with depression and anger. Counseling and workshops are available where you can learn to access your own anger in a safe environment, learn about your own history with anger, and start to understand why you feel so uncomfortable expressing yourself in this way.

Opening to our own internal conflict and wrath helps us transform the forces of darkness into illumination. This is the path towards facing our deepest subconscious fears and freeing ourselves of their power over us, thus changing negative energy into insight. By honestly working on our own human failings, we may eventually transform them into inherent wisdom.

To be healthy human beings we must have access to *all of our emotions*. When we are abused or treated unfairly, and our anger surfaces, we must feel free to show a strong defensive response, making it crystal clear that this is not acceptable behavior. Protecting ourselves and our right to be who we are is the beginning of true self-responsibility, self-empowerment, and self-respect.

Healing from within:
Core corrections

*The hardest battle you will face in life is to be
no one but yourself in a world which is trying its
hardest to make you like everybody else.*

It is now time to get down to the real healing process. Although there are millions of personal stories about shame and disillusionment with love, the issues we each struggle with are basic and fundamental.

Most of the insecurity and low self-esteem in the world is caused by rejection by a parent, boyfriend/girlfriend, husband/wife, or the loss of a parent or some other significant other early in life. Early shame, rejection, or abandonment may have become internalized at an early age, making us feel worthless and unworthy of love. The greatest loss and the most difficult to work through is the death of a parent.

After we suffer early trauma, our fear of further loss may become so great that we avoid true closeness with others altogether. We may overcome childhood setbacks, even go on to earn impressive graduate degrees and excel in our career goals. From the outside we may appear to be the picture of success, but inside we know we are not content with ourselves and our lives. Those first emotional wounds from early trauma remain seething inside, unhealed and unhealthy.

Contrary to popular belief, time does not heal all wounds. Raw, deep, painful experiences do not simply disappear from memory. They hide deep inside and continue to undermine our ability to maintain intimate relationships. We can be attractive, intelligent, loving, and kind, but vivid memories of betrayal and heartbreak continue to cause painful trust issues. Our wounds are there to protect us, but instead they keep us in our own versions of solitary confinement. We are not free to open up to others in healthy ways or develop robust, meaningful personal lives.

Seen from the outside, an individual may not appear to have abandonment or trust issues. They may have relationships and even marry, but deep inside they know they have never found the kind of compassion and respect they seek from themselves, or the understanding and safety they seek in relationships with others. Consequently they will continue to choose inappropriate partners, relationships that reinforce previous assumptions about how love is not available to them because they are fundamentally worthless and unloveable. In fact, most who have suffered rejection and abandonment feel unworthy of love. They see it as something others have special access to, but never them.

More commonly, they will spend at least half of their lives not realizing what's missing, because their standards are so low. They may feel they only deserve the kind of love they experienced in their upbringing or early years, defining love in that way, and never realizing what they are missing. Asking for more seems unrealistic or selfish. But as they work on their self-esteem and gain higher levels of self-respect, they finally see how low their standards really are.

How do we push through to attract higher levels of love and respect? The only way is by changing ourselves from the inside out. By finding the necessary support and then taking the time and emotional energy to access all the guilt, shame, and doubt from our pasts, we can be reborn with new faith in following our hearts to new and improved forms of love.

This is a do-it-yourself job

It may be tempting to think that reading the right books or finding the right therapist or counselor will change you. Although it is essential that you choose carefully and trust your inner wisdom in selecting the guides who can assist you best in this deep, emotional process, you are the only one who can create real change in your life. You must take full responsibility for changing your life and your perspective on love, and be willing to do the hard work necessary to create deep personal change.

Spiritual work is not something you can copy from someone else and expect the same results. The spiritual work needed by each of us is quite unique to our own spiritual needs, determined by where we have been harmed in our individual pasts. It's like attending an aerobics class to slim down. Others may be doing the same or similar moves, but if you aren't sensitive to your own needs, you won't gain the benefits you seek.

Too many of us think we can simply purchase the right book and change our perspective. That's probably why we buy so many self-help books. Read a book and change your life! Although I applaud the fact that you are aware enough to know you need to change, let me reemphasize the fact that real personal change only comes about through some serious emotional heavy lifting. What is that? It is spending time alone taking a hard look at yourself, at how you have treated yourself and others, and at how you have brought yourself to this difficult point in your life. Then it requires taking full self-responsibility from here on out.

Taking 100% self-responsibility is one of the most important steps towards genuine self-love and self-respect. When we take less than 100% self-responsibility, we operate from the victim role. (Take care of me, I'm inadequate.) When we try to take more than 100% responsibility we are operating from the rescuer role. Most of us do not have the power to rescue anyone else. Taking full self-responsibility means saving yourself, the only one you truly have the power to save.

Responsibility is best taken as a celebration rather than as a burden. It is a freeing act. Taking responsibility for ourselves takes back power over our own happiness. Childhood is over. We can only take action in this moment. Instead of focusing on what somebody did to you in the past, you must now focus on what you want to create in your future. No more blaming or shaming others. Are you playing the victim or the rescuer in your life right now?

Here are some helpful affirmations for taking full self-responsibility:

- I am completely responsible for all my own feelings and actions.
- I am completely responsible for my own health and welfare.
- I give others complete responsibility for their feelings and actions.
- I take complete responsibility for making and keeping agreements, no excuses!
- I take responsibility for expressing my true essence in the world in positive and loving ways.

Yes, changing your feelings about yourself and your life requires a major effort on your part. It can take years and usually involves some gut-wrenching experiences, but I'm here to say it is possible to change your perspective on yourself and others. Personal change can and does happen, and it is always worth the effort.

Learning how to focus on your own unique trust issues

If you have done your work in the areas of regaining self-love and self-respect, dealt with some of your own personal trust and anger issues, and confronted the fact that you must stop blaming and shaming yourself and others when you feel inadequate, it is now time to seriously consider why you don't believe in love.

Your own specific life experiences may have created a private and unique love dilemma for you. Shame and trust issues from childhood may have played a part, so be certain not to underplay or minimize past trauma. Spend time alone thinking, feeling, and journaling about what is now standing in your way. What needs to happen next for you to move on?

What were your deepest emotional reactions to your first experiments with romantic love? Did you only attract challenging or abusive relationships? What did you learn about yourself along the way? Did you feel unsafe or inadequate? Did you dissociate or withdraw emotionally at some point because your first experiences with love ended so badly? How have you coped through the years? Have you just avoided the subject, even though you know how much you crave intimacy in your life? Do you now understand how early disappointments around love can retraumatize us, throwing us back into primary shame and fundamental self-worth issues? How long ago did you first lose your faith in love as a positive force in your life?

What might help you work back to your core issues so that a real sense of healing can occur? When something traumatic and incomprehensible happens to us, we naturally want to understand it and find our way back to feeling some sort of order in things. What answers do you need from your past so that you can begin anew, with a whole new perspective on love? What do you need to know or understand better to move from disillusionment to a new belief that love can transform your life into something better?

One essential tool you may never have fully utilized is your inner wisdom or intuition. It is now time to use one of your most powerful tools to change your life.

Accessing your intuition: Listening to a new kind of wisdom

We cannot solve problems by using the same kind of thinking we used when we created them.

~Albert Einstein

Can we change, and if so, how? We can only change with renewed self-awareness, honest self-love, determination, positive support from others, the addition of a few new skill sets, and with a willingness to go inside of ourselves to harvest the wisdom we have accumulated over a lifetime. All of this takes courage.

Determination and courage come from the absolute certainty that the way we have been living so far has not worked. When you reach that desperate moment when you know your rational mind no longer has all of the answers you seek, it is time to surrender. Admitting surrender is difficult. This admission is equivalent to acknowledging that you have failed in your efforts so far. Pure stubbornness and denial of your feelings and needs have not given you the life you had hoped for, or the answers you seek. You would be crazy to continue on this path.

Now what? It is now time to welcome in the wisdom of the universe and those others who wish to help. It is now time to begin to access the wisdom of your own intuition, every little whisper emanating from your unconscious, your dreams, or wherever they come from. These are the voices that will guide you back to where you so want to go.

Intuition is tricky. It is a way of knowing, yet it is often unclear how we know. Some seem to have greater natural access to their intuition, but we all can develop the necessary skills to access this invaluable inner guidance. Extrasensory perception, clairvoyance, and telepathy are all different types of intuitive access to your right brain, the hemisphere that specializes in intuitive, holistic pattern perceptions. Most of us have been raised to strongly value messages from our rational, linear left brain. It is now time to listen to the other side of the story and find some brain balance.

Why bother? Because by combining the power of your own intuition with your intellect, you will begin to see different patterns and recognize new possibilities, opening up your mind to many new choices that were not available to you before. Intuition is an essential tool to guide you towards a healthier sense of yourself and an understanding of what you need to do next to attract what you want into your life. For some excellent instruction in accessing the power of your own intuition, you may want to read *Awakening Intuition* by Frances E. Vaughan, a psychologist who specializes in integrating psychology and spiritual growth. She states:

> Awakening intuition enables one to see the choices available and is thus a liberating experience. . . . At any given moment one is conscious of only a small portion of what one knows. Intuition allows one to draw on that vast storehouse of unconscious knowledge that includes not only everything that one has experienced or learned, either consciously or subliminally, but also the infinite reservoir of the collective and universal unconscious.

Do you believe it is possible to expand your consciousness to include your intuitive side? Do you believe you could benefit from an expansion of your level of self-awareness? If you do not believe this is possible, then it probably isn't. Don't lie to yourself about what you believe. If you simply feel perplexed or confused, acknowledge that is where you are right now. Welcome in all of your disillusioned parts to participate in this experiment in accessing the rest of your brain, the part that hasn't been available to help for all these years.

Quiet the mind of its perpetual chatter. Relax so you may learn how to listen to what you already know inside. You may need to take some time alone to access these new caring voices. They are hard to hear if the rest of your life is in chaos. Trust in your inner wisdom to show you what steps you need to take to open previously closed doors and learn why you are not open to love now.

How intuition worked for me

When I first started accessing my own intuition, I was surprised to realize how many layers there were. My intuition chose to speak to me in many different voices, usually when I was facing some stressful change or condition, one I had never faced before and had no idea how to handle. I knew I was in over my head, so I opened to any suggestions from my intellect and my intuition.

Messages commonly come to me when I first wake up from my dreams. Sometimes I will wake up with a dream or the words from a particular song on my mind, and when I explore the meaning in more depth, I see the unique message meant specifically for me. It sometimes feels like a small miracle, this access to my inner guide, my own special way of knowing what I should do next.

Some ask me how I know these messages come specifically from my intuition and are not just random ideas or thoughts. In my own case, my intuition comes through loud and clear, telling me to go meet this person, read this book, or see this movie now. Or to get away from that person. The only question is whether I will choose to listen and obey or instead will ignore its suggestions. In a crisis, most of my intuitive guidance comes through in dreams or song lyrics.

One aspect of my most important intuitive messages is that they refuse to be ignored. They don't give up, but keep coming until I do what they say. My intuition can be very stubborn at times, and when I follow through with the action required, I am rewarded exquisitely!

As you get better at listening, the messages become clearer and more distinguishable. It's just another skill to add to your repertoire of living skills, but this one is important because there are times when intuitive messages can be essential in making crucial life decisions. I will never forget the message I received on the day I learned I would be losing my job. I was very upset when I got in my car to drive home. Just as I got on the highway, a voice came through loud and clear. It said, "This will probably save your life!"

My entire process—first, acknowledging that I had lost my faith in love, and then, finding that faith again—was guided by my newfound trust in my own intuition. As I began to explore my apparent lack of faith in love, I noticed a tinge of cynicism. My intuition told me I should go read my old journals from decades past. Because I had had a traumatic experience with rejection from a lover at age 24, I read my journals to remind myself what had really happened, because I knew how memories can be unreliable over time. Every time we take out an old memory and look at it, we fiddle with it just a bit, so the past does not conflict with our present assessment of reality.

On a deep level I then realized that the only way I would finally be able to resolve so many painful feelings from my past was to talk to my ex-lover. This led eventually to an absolutely undeniable urge to try to open up communications with a lover I hadn't spoken to in over 25 years.

The thought of casually giving him a call felt crazy and irrational. I tried my best to tell my intuition to be quiet. Contacting an old lover felt like a complete contradiction of what my rational mind would advise. Why would I call up someone who had rejected me decades before? This seemed like masochistic behavior.

But my intuition persisted. Finally I wrote him a simple letter of inquiry, asking how he was doing. When he hadn't responded in a year, I became angry and my intuition jumped in again. This time I wrote a more honest letter, explaining why I had had so much trouble getting past our breakup back in 1978. I knew on some level I needed some honest answers from him before I could completely let go of my feelings of betrayal and anger from our shared past.

My intuition was also behind my decision to start a matchmaking service after I lost my job as a librarian. I felt crazy, but also somehow certain that I needed to follow through with this unlikely pursuit. My friends can all attest to my confusion. It seemed like a quantum leap from being a practical, responsible academic librarian to a freelance matchmaker. For as long as I could I fought back against my apparently irrational urge to go into matchmaking, but my intuition begged to differ. My inner voice insisted that I needed to watch the movie *Risky Business*. Although I hadn't a clue why, I finally gave in and watched it. The reasons why I needed to see this movie then became crystal clear.

The teenagers in the movie are trying to decide whether to start their own "risky business." Then one wise teenage character says, "Every now and then you need to say what the f*** and make your move! What the f*** brings you freedom. Freedom brings opportunity. Opportunity makes your future." After watching that scene in the movie, I trusted my gut, took their advice, and went ahead with my own version of a risky business.

Through my matchmaking service I met many others who were disillusioned with their own love histories, and this made me feel much better about myself. It showed me I was not alone in my desire to find my way back to love, and I wasn't crazy either. All of my clients had various levels of ambivalence about believing in love again.

Interviewing the men was quite instructional to me. It showed me that there are plenty of attractive, funny, intelligent, authentic single men with integrity, men who feel as perplexed as the rest of us when it comes to love. They were also dealing with the confusing dilemma of starting to date again in their 40s and 50s.

Getting to know so many cool, older love seekers, and talking in depth to them, finally gave me the extra courage I needed to give my ex-lover a call. I knew in my heart that I needed a few crucial answers that only he could provide. I had unresolved pain and anger that had accumulated over the years, resulting in what seemed like an insurmountable obstacle in the path of my renewed belief in love. I knew intuitively that the question of what had happened between us, and why, was something I needed to understand before I could truly forgive myself and move on to a powerful new belief in a higher love.

My body/mind wisdom was pushing me unconsciously towards an essential catharsis that would purge me of all the shame and pain from my past relationships, paving the way to a renewed belief in the power of love to transform my life.

Catharsis: A unique way to create powerful and lasting change

Action is the greatest antidote to despair. ~Joan Baez

The word *catharsis* is derived from the Greek word meaning cleansing or purification. Most definitions include the idea of strong emotional processing leading to a powerful insight as a result of some important unconscious realization becoming suddenly conscious. The American Psychological Association defines it as "the discharge of affects connected to traumatic events that had previously been repressed, by bringing these events back into consciousness and reexperiencing them."

Although it may manifest in very different ways, the essence of catharsis remains the same: a release from some emotional burden, which furthers healing through its cleansing effect. Aristotle said that watching a tragedy had a corrective and healing effect. He believed that catharsis helped to moderate strong emotions, therefore restoring the balance in one's heart. The effects of surprise are key factors that lead to catharsis.

Current research in psychology supports the hypothesis that significant change is possible when powerful emotional connections are combined with cognitive reframing and reeducation. New models of emotional development suggest that emotions play an important "binding" role in memory, so that reenactments of traumatic life experiences may be a way of elevating memory-bound emotions into conscious awareness, where they can be effectively worked with.

Catharsis is often used in theater and movie scripts, capturing that deeply emotional moment when the main character sees the mistakes from his or her past and experiences dramatic and sudden personal change. We humans seek and enjoy activities that help us symbolically relive our own painful emotional experiences at a safe distance, thus achieving some sense of relief or resolution.

A good example of theatrical catharsis comes at the end of Shakespeare's play *Romeo and Juliet*. The tragic death of these two innocent young lovers often reawakens feelings of loss in the viewers and allows them to find relief by reliving unfinished personal loss in their own lives.

Historically, catharsis has been used as a powerful part of most religious or spiritual experience. The act of revealing painful or guilt-ridden thoughts so that one can then feel purified is a part of most rituals of baptism and confession. Confession involves the recall, revelation, and release of forbidden thoughts, actions, and repressed emotions. These types of spiritual and cultural rituals help people process collective stressors such as illness, death, and other major life-changing events, thus releasing the emotions related to those stressors. Traditionally, ceremonies of mourning, funeral rites, and curing rituals often include cathartic activities such as crying, drumming, or ecstatic dance.

With the use of many social media opportunities on the Internet, adults worldwide have begun reconnecting with lovers from decades past. Many stories have emerged of high school and college sweethearts who had married others and gone on with their lives, only to reconnect later in life. In some cases, love is reborn through these connections. In other cases, an excellent opportunity is provided for a deeper understanding of past relationships, which can lead to a much-needed cathartic release.

My own experience with intuitive catharsis

One bright July morning, I finally decided to give my old lover a call. Twenty-five years after our last conversation, he sounded familiar, friendly, and fabulous. He even seemed pleased to hear from me! We had always found it easy to talk with each other, and that hadn't changed. We spoke for a couple of hours about how we had changed in the past 25 years, what we had learned, and how we had grown. At the end of the conversation he said, "Thanks for calling—you made my day!"

We continued to talk over the next month or so, and I slowly fell back in love with him. At first, I held out hope that love might rekindle between us. But as we spoke, I realized this was not the reason for our renewed bond. For decades I had felt deep and enduring shame about how our relationship had ended, blaming myself for the failure of our love affair back in our early twenties. He now told me the truth, how severe depression had ruined his relationships and ruled his life. He apologized for the trauma he had caused in mine.

Talking to him was quite reassuring. Our conversations were exactly what I needed to finally completely heal my broken heart from decades past. I now had a much more complete understanding of what had happened between us 25 years earlier, with an absolute certainty I had not squandered the best love relationship I had ever had. Bless him for having the patience and courage to share his truth with me and listen to my accumulated anguish over past rejection. Our talks unearthed decades of excruciating personal pain, which then flowed out in one gigantic, cathartic wave of relief. I finally felt healed from decades of self-blame and ready to take a chance on love again.

Limitations and restrictions when it comes to catharsis

Cathartic methods are not for everybody. Individuals who have difficulty expressing emotions may be helped more than those who are already expressive or over-expressive. For those with extra emotional challenges like Borderline Personality Disorder, dissociation disorders, or some mood disorders, catharsis may not be appropriate without individual work on ego strength and emotional-control skills and without strong support networks.

The special challenges of believing in love again after a divorce

Beauty is the garden where hope grows.

There were many things I enjoyed about the personal-transformation film *Under the Tuscan Sun* back in 2003. Much like the Diane Lane character, I also transformed my life completely after suffering a devastating divorce in 2001. First I moved away from my ex, and then I began the physical experience of renovating a house. Beginning in the backyard, I learned some of the lessons only nurturing a garden can provide. And then the major overhaul began!

One line from *Under the Tuscan Sun* stuck with me: "It's amazing that divorce does not kill you." Two things amazed me about the death of my first marriage. One was that I could feel so bad at the breakup, even though I was completely sick and tired of non-stop blaming and shaming from my husband. In retrospect, I named the marriage Criticism Central, and my ex the King of Blame. Part of my process was to acknowledge that my ex and I hadn't been all that close during our marriage. When we wed, we were both 39, and I realize only now how we both kept our distance to some extent, unconsciously preparing for the demise of our relationship from the very beginning.

My second surprise was my husband's apparent lack of emotion around the entire experience. He was always very practical and a "money man" (entrepreneur, MBA). He seemed to see the death of our marital partnership as a great time to reorganize his money. He showed me no emotions whatsoever.

Now I have learned more about the major differences between male and female responses to emotionally difficult times. In her book *The Female Brain*, Dr. Louann Brizendine says being present with difficult emotions is hardwired into women, but not something most men deal with well. For most women, the end of their marriage can feel like the end of their world, and yet it is not uncommon for men to confront this major life change with complete indifference.

The greatest revelation I had from my divorce was how inappropriate our pairing had been to begin with. We learn so much more from divorcing a person than we could have ever learned from marrying them. When divorce starts to rear its ugly head, the gloves come off and we all stop playing nice.

How could I have ever imagined, when I first saw *Under the Tuscan Sun* in 2003, that in just a few short years I would finally find the man I'd been looking for my entire life, one who was willing to commit completely to our future together.

This is the deeper lesson of divorce or any painful transition in our lives. With time and much work on yourself some wounds do heal, we learn so much about ourselves by going through this process, and there is always hope that a much better life is just around the corner.

Let's face it. Being eternally angry at your ex is the great American pastime. Have you ever considered all of the angry, ugly feelings that surround us constantly, as half of all American adults break up their marriages and then try to find a way to get even with each other? There's a lot of ugliness out there, and it is all negative energy that is helping nobody get what they want out of life.

The only way to convert all of that negativity into something good is to forgive yourself for being human. As a human being you have made a mistake. Now you are ready to learn much more about who you are and how you can stop making the same type of mistake in your future.

Under your anger is seemingly boundless pain and frustration. Anger is what we show the world, but the pain is also under there somewhere. Underneath it all is a small child who made a bargain to be loved, appreciated, and understood and now feels absolute betrayal. You trusted the wrong person with your heart, your dreams, and your sense of self, and this person bashed them to bits. What now?

A long period of grieving is in order. Do whatever it takes to love yourself now. Take long walks alone or with friends, get back into those hobbies you used to enjoy, get a loving pet or two who will show you boundless, abiding loyalty, and write in your journal about how unfair life has been to you. Listen to music and watch movies that help you feel better about yourself.

Get angry at your ex, but realize you are actually also quite angry at yourself. You gave your power away to someone who did not appreciate you. Perhaps s/he didn't even have the potential to love at all. Do not believe all those negative things your ex may say about you. After a year or two you may feel the need to fully acknowledge how destructive your ex was to your own self-image. By spending so much time with someone who had so little respect for all of the wonderful things that you are, you have lost your way. It is now time to build your self-respect back up.

Getting rid of negative beliefs about yourself: A case study

It is now time for me to fully acknowledge how destructive and abusive my ex has been in my life. I've just realized how negative his influence is even now, a couple of years later. He seems to be moving on with his life, and I guess it's high time I do the same.

The two useless beliefs I gained from spending too much time married to him are:

Men are all jerks.

No one will ever want to be with me, because I'm too much trouble.

With his constant criticism and harassment, he somehow convinced me that I am flawed in some important ways and unable to love or be loved. I now feel so angry that I gave him that much power and influence over me and how I feel about myself. When we first met, he said he feared no one would ever want to spend time with him. Now, instead, he has convinced me that I am not worth spending time with.

When I think about all of the criticism I faced daily from him, about everything from the way I dressed to the way I blew my nose, I feel so angry! Why did I stay so long? What is the matter with me? I feel so flawed. How will I ever feel loveable again?

Taking your power back from your ex

As long as your ex holds any power over even one choice or decision you make today, s/he still holds power over you. Do not allow the death of your relationship or your marriage to represent the death of all you can now be, or your own ability to believe in love again. You must now rebuild your own sense of self-love and self-respect, beyond any feelings you may still have about your ex. And this time you will learn to love this new you more than ever before, so much so that no one will ever have the power to destroy you emotionally again.

When one thing ends, another begins, but this time it will be different. This time your ability to love others will be based on a solid foundation of self-love and self-respect. No one will ever be negative or abusive towards you for long, because you will be long gone if they do.

Do not allow your ex to hold any power over the decisions you make today. After grieving the loss of the dream of what your past love might have been, put some serious time into relearning who you are and what you have to offer this world. Find the certainty within yourself that you are now ready to go on and find something better. Then give yourself a gigantic hug of compassion for trying so hard and fighting the good fight.

For a few years after my separation and divorce, I tortured myself ruthlessly for my own failings. I blamed myself for the failure of my marriage and also for the fact that I had stayed in an emotionally abusive relationship for far too long. I kept asking myself, *"Why did you do that? You have a career and options. Why did you accept his emotional sabotage for so long?"*

I still don't know all of the answers to those questions. Part of the answer was my own stubborn desire to "make" my marriage work. I now see that I never held that power in the first place. For a marriage to give each member the will to continue, it takes two adults working together with a moment-to-moment commitment to authentic communication, self-responsibility, and a deep appreciation of all the benefits offered by the relationship.

It no longer surprises me that more than half of all marriages fail. Most of us do not have the level of maturity and self-respect needed to sustain an authentic, positive, and loving relationship over the long haul. To learn to understand and appreciate this unique human being you have committed to, "through thick and thin, in sickness and in health," is a lot to ask from any of us.

We all have our difficult moments when all seems lost or hopeless. We all have times when our loved one doesn't seem all that loveable. The way I relate to these moments is to appreciate the fact that I also find myself fundamentally unloveable at times. How do I respond to these feelings within myself? Do I hate myself? Sometimes, but more and more I now work to find compassion for myself and my daily struggles. The more easily I can find compassion for myself, the easier I am to live with.

The way I measure my present relationships is to constantly ask myself this simple question: "Does relating to this person *give me energy* or *take it away?*" I have become sensitive to the energy dynamics in all of my dealings with myself and others.

Some friends free my soul. They help me get excited about all the possibilities in life and encourage me to keep growing and changing and becoming a better me. These friends feel like my personal cheerleaders. I know they believe in me and I believe in them implicitly.

Mike, the man I met after I began to believe in love again, is my best cheerleader. He understands my struggles and my need to be alone at times, but he *never stops loving and believing in me.* He never loses faith in the power of our combined spirits, and I try to always do the same for him. With authenticity, respect, and appreciation we continue on. And, of course, with boundless love!

Transforming negative thought patterns: Don't believe everything you think!

Learn how to treat yourself at least as well as you treat others in your life.

Why do we keep re-creating the same realities for ourselves? Why do we repeat the same mistakes in our relationships with others? It is because all too often we believe everything we think.

The first step in changing internally limiting mental patterns is to understand exactly how your brain works. New discoveries in the brain sciences suggest that you can take control of your mind instead of letting it control you. It is estimated that the human brain has about 100 billion neurons and 100 trillion synapses. Each one of our neurons may be connected to hundreds of other brain cells by as many as 10,000 synapses. The average person thinks between 12,000 to 50,000 thoughts per day, most of which are not even conscious. Every conscious and unconscious thought we think is used by the same network of brain cells and synapses—every single time.

When we have a thought, that thought attracts similar thoughts, because neural electrical branches grow secondary branches leading to similar thoughts, and our brains have a tendency to hold on to those thoughts we think most often.

What happens in our brains determines what happens in our lives. That's why we need to stop believing everything we think. Subconscious thoughts come to us effortlessly because the synapses that give life to them are wider and information can pass through them more easily. They often represent the sights and sounds from our past that we have mentally revisited the most often or that have affected us on the deepest emotional level—whether positive or negative.

One of the worst difficulties any of us can cope with is being haunted by negative thoughts that constantly repeat themselves, seemingly without our conscious control.

Negative unconscious thoughts from our childhoods are particularly brutal because they are the most deeply ingrained. We tend to believe these messages and then let them define who we are in every life situation. Fortunately, we now know that we have the power to choose which thoughts to develop and which to eliminate.

If you are indeed serious about transforming your life and your feelings about finding love, the first step is to change the way you think about yourself. It is now time to challenge all of your previous assumptions about who you are and why you do the things you do. Begin by consciously choosing thoughts that are the complete opposite of your usual negative patterns.

Just by repeatedly thinking something positive about yourself, something you want to think, on a daily basis, you can make your negative thoughts disappear. Positive thoughts will then affect your habitual emotions, your self-identifying belief systems, and your interactions with others.

The most well-known positive thoughts are called affirmations. I'm sure you've heard of these. If you decide to fill your mind with positive, chosen thoughts to replace the negative self-talk you've been focused on since childhood or since some traumatic incident in your life, the negative thought patterns will slowly begin to appear incorrect. My favorite affirmation is:

"I love you and respect you exactly the way you are!"

Stand in front of a mirror, look yourself directly in the eyes, and say this a few times a day until it feels true and natural.

Another way to challenge previous negative brain patterns is to begin questioning deeply your feelings about specific situations in your life. When you are involved in a difficult situation or feeling bad about a belief about yourself, first write it down. Then separate yourself from the emotions of the situation and begin to dive deeper into the root of your unhappiness.

Play the "why" game. For example, you might say, "Thinking about this time in my life makes me feel bad about myself." Then ask yourself why. If your answer is, "Because I feel guilty (stupid, selfish)," keep asking yourself why. In only a few cycles of why's you will begin to access your true feelings in much more depth. Getting down to your real feelings about a situation may help you give yourself a break about some past behavior. Your goal is a deeper understanding of yourself and your motivations and a feeling of self-compassion.

The joys of solitude

*Just when the caterpillar thought the world was
over, it became a butterfly.*

While leading a workshop, I asked the women in the group
to share a few of their fears. One woman, a 50-something di-
vorcée, did not hesitate. She responded, "I'm afraid to grow old
without a companion."

The truth is, if this woman does remain single, she'll soon
have plenty of company. As we baby-boomer women age, more
and more of us will find ourselves alone. Some of us will never
marry. Others will divorce. And statistically speaking, the majority of wives end up widows.

If all this sounds depressing, keep in mind that being single
isn't the same as being alone, and being alone isn't the same
as being lonely. Some of the loneliest people on the planet are
married.

When asked if she envies her married friends, one divorced
client said, "Not really. Many of my married friends feel as unhappy and isolated as I was when I was married. Yes, I'd prefer
to have a partner, but I needed to be on my own to become
myself. I like who I am so much better now."

That has been my exact experience throughout my life.
Sure, I had my fearful, lonely times, especially after I divorced
and then lost my job. But I also realized on some level the gift
I had been handed: time alone to explore who I had become
and decide what was next for me.

That kind of freedom from outside responsibilities is essential for going deep and then resurfacing as a brand-new
person, the person you are inside. Afterwards, I spent time

getting reacquainted with the new me, to appreciate all I had become. I decided I loved what I saw, and then, only months after that, I met a man who felt exactly the same way.

Going solo for periods of your life can be challenging, and yet so emotionally productive. Spending quality time alone to dig deep into your soul and connect with your true self takes time and much emotional energy. I like the term "soul surgery." It also takes courage, lots of it! But the results can change you into the person you have always been inside, your best self.

Substantive solitude is the best way to find out who you really are and what you value now. Who knows what you might discover. I encourage you to take the risk!

To learn more about the gifts of solitude and aloneness, please read *The Call of Solitude: Alonetime in a World of Attachment* by Ester Schaler Buchholz.

What does love mean to me now?

Love is not just something that happens to you. It is
a certain special way of being alive. ~Thomas Merton

Love is first and foremost self-love and acceptance. It is openness, honesty, and the excitement of knowing that if we put ourselves out there exactly as we are, some will find us absolutely irresistible.

Love is also not the same in every decade of our lives. When we are young it often comes from a place of boundless insecurity. "Who would ever love me?" And then, "I'm so glad someone finds me loveable!"

We love less selfishly as we age. By slowly gaining a strong sense of self-love and confidence we finally realize and acknowledge that we do indeed have a lot to offer as a partner in love and life. We may start to appreciate certain aspects of ourselves. "Gee, I really am a funny person." Or, "I have a lot to offer in terms of intelligence and sensitivity."

How does love become "a certain special way of being alive"? What does this look and feel like from the inside looking out? To me it is an attitude of openness. It is learning how to finally, authentically let go of past rejection and disappointment, and then step outside of your comfort zone just enough to trust others again. That includes the challenge of first taking the time and energy to become your best self, and then having the courage to show your authentic self to the world with new confidence. The challenge is in knowing exactly who you are, and then being willing to take the risk that others will find as much enjoyment in your presence as you do.

The first time I met Mike, my second husband, I felt like I was taking a gigantic risk by simply being myself. And yet if I had not taken that risk, how would we have known how wonderfully compatible we immediately were?

That is why I strongly recommend that those meeting new friends through online dating sites first take the time to love and accept yourself exactly as you are, and then express that clearly when you first meet others. It does not serve the purposes of either one of you to camouflage your true self in armoring or disguise. You can only look forward to future disappointment and disillusionment when the truth comes out.

I had great respect for Mike's decision to immediately discuss his recent struggles with a difficult, misunderstood chronic illness. Before we ever met, he told me about his life with chronic fatigue syndrome. He knew he didn't want to get involved with a woman who was not able to deal with this daily reality. That this man would be so honest with a total stranger caused me to feel immediate trust.

Daily ways to increase your faith
and confidence in love

"I'm terrified of hope!"

Everywhere I go I meet so many interesting and *cool* older singles who are losing hope in ever finding true love again. My advice to them: **Don't give up!** By running a matchmaking service for older singles, I learned how many cool adults are looking for love later in life. More than you could possibly imagine!

Your best proof that you could meet someone great *today* is this simple fact: You are single and look how amazing you are! There must be others just like you wondering how to connect with other singles. Why not begin erring on the side of optimism, and find a way to believe in love again?

Have you ever heard the expression, Whatever you focus on grows? Instead of giving up in your own mind and heart, instead of convincing yourself to lose your faith in love, try putting your heart and soul behind the idea that the love of your life is just around the corner!

I know of what I speak. Probably *nobody* could have convinced me, the day I met Mike six years ago, that I was about to meet the man I had been hoping to meet forever. But I had been putting my heart and soul out there for quite a while before it happened.

First of all, I *did* start a dating service. I did spend lots of time interviewing eligible women and men. And I even took what felt like a gigantic risk when I called a past lover to clear out my love drain pipes from past disappointment and pain.

How could you prepare to meet the love of your life today? How could you focus more positively on how it will feel when you *know* you've just met *the one*? How could you work today on removing all the obstacles in your brain and heart to believing that this could really happen?

I have a suggestion. Before I met Mike, I made a point of watching movies and listening to music that were totally positive about love. That's one way to consciously control your own brain waves. I saw it as a sign when great love songs came on the radio. I can highly recommend most Stevie Wonder songs, but my own personal favorite is "Higher Love" by Steve Winwood. In fact his whole album *Back in the High Life* is the essence of positive love vibes.

Make some small investment today in your future happiness by watching the movies and TV shows and listening to the music that make you feel great—you know, the way it feels to be in love!

Online dating dos and don'ts

While perusing the *Huffington Post* recently, I came upon an interesting advice column apparently directed at those in their twenties. It asked if "digital dating" was only for "desperate, older people."

This was a whole new concept for me. Did you know that youngsters today are embarrassed to admit that they've considered or tried online dating? This column was an attempt to encourage young people to not feel as if online dating were only for "pathetic older people."

Are we all feeling pathetic or "older" out there? No, because we're smart enough to know that meeting the right partner is only one of the greatest challenges in life, especially after you're out in the real world with a mortgage, kids, and a million other things on your mind.

I have to say I never felt desperate, pathetic, or older when I turned to eHarmony.com or Match.com. I felt realistic. I worked in an academic library with women and mostly gay men, and I hadn't met a man I was attracted to in years!

I happen to believe that online dating is no different from any other type of dating. You just need to approach it with the right attitude and be clear about your goals. Do not expect Prince Charming, unless of course you are Princess Charming. Expect to meet ordinary, flawed human beings just like yourself, who believe that their lives could be much improved with some positive, loving companionship.

Life is tough enough on your own, feeling responsible for everything that could go wrong in your world. Why not look around for someone to share the ups and downs with?

I'm just happy that there is this new and sometimes improved method of meeting those in your area who might mesh with you and your needs. Just remember it's "Safety First" when getting back into dating.

First of all, do not begin dating until you are completely ready. Until then, go out with friends, get massages, or go dancing for the pleasures of physical touching, and find close friends of both genders who will be on your side no matter what.

Go out and do activities you really enjoy where you might meet others who like the same activities you do. Do not try to fool others by doing something you hate just to meet people. Be authentic in all of your efforts to meet similarly minded others.

If you wish, try online dating, but keep in mind that people lie about their height, age, looks, finances, marital status, and emotional stability. Have fun but don't believe everything you read or hear!

Be completely honest in your own online profile. If you lie by putting outdated photos online or lie about something obvious like your height and weight, those you meet will know immediately that you are a dishonest person and begin to wonder what else you lied about.

Don't e-mail or talk on the phone more than a few times before meeting in person. It is far too easy to project onto this person you haven't ever met, making him or her your ideal mate in cyberspace. When you do finally meet, you will both be even more disappointed. Be yourself and get in the room with a real human being as soon as possible, before your imagination goes wild.

Don't make your first date a "real" date. No matter how intimate you may feel from e-mails or phone conversations, remember this is a complete stranger you're meeting. The first time, meet for coffee or a walk in a public place where you can talk. No noisy bars, no endless dinner, and don't extend or accept any invitations to each other's house until you know each other well.

When you do go out on a real date, be sure a friend knows where you're going and with whom. Call your buddy when you get home.

When you're ready to have *sex* again, use condoms every time. It's a hassle, sure, but it's a myth that only young people are at risk for HIV and other STDs.

What are your odds of finding love again?

I would say the odds depend entirely on you.

First of all, you need to redefine love for yourself. What are your expectations? What would love look like or feel like now? I highly recommend writing down a list of your own desires and deal breakers. But the most important determining factor at this point is whether you still believe in love.

Chances are, if you are recently separated or divorced, you still have lots of bad feelings lurking about love. Love may just seem like a bad joke, filled with betrayal, anger, and bitterness.

In my case, a 25-year-old ache returned after I left my husband. I slowly realized that I had never really gotten over a love affair gone wrong in my early 20s. That sense of betrayal still haunted me in two ways. First of all, it was my first experience with what I thought was a healthy, positive love affair, so the rejection came as an absolute shock. And I could not get beyond the guilt I felt for somehow ruining the best love relationship of my entire life. Having such an early and disillusioning love experience lowered my standards for all future relationships. I felt like I couldn't expect too much in my future.

I felt a deep need to understand my past love disillusionments before I could move on and believe again. My own dilemma was how to find peace with my past so I could begin to believe again. After much soul-searching and many tears, I decided the only real solution for me was to talk to the man who had hurt me many years before. He held the key to my catharsis.

Do you have any dark, painful issues lurking in your own love history that have created false beliefs and expectations of what love is or can be?

After I resolved my past issues, I became determined to find someone who loved me exactly the way I was. I found a new belief that love was possible and even likely. I wanted someone who could become my best cheerleader in life, and I felt certain I could offer the same to him, because I again believed in the power of love.

Because of advertising and some wild cultural values, we have this crazy idea that love has to do with how we look and what we wear. But deep down inside we are all like children, craving true acceptance and understanding.

I learned that if you can find a way to truly believe in love again, and give yourself renewed self-compassion, others will find you much more loveable!

The five stages of romantic relationships

Love is plunging into darkness toward a place that
may exist.   ~Marge Piercy

Love just happens to be one of the most studied subjects
around. Sometimes I wish I had known at least some of these
things back in the 1970s when I was first falling in love. Based
on many models proposed by psychologists, therapists, re-
searchers, and clinicians, here is a hybrid look at the typical
journey of a committed relationship—keeping in mind that
every relationship follows its own path:

Infatuation

This is the Hollywood version of romantic love. It's the but-
terflies in the stomach and the fluttery heart that feels ever
so good.

There is an emphasis on finding similarities between each
other and glossing over differences. There is a tendency to
idealize the other person. There is a high degree of passion
and the (unrealistic) expectation that this person will be able
to satisfy all needs and wants.

Each person tends to think of the other person constantly.
A scientific explanation suggests why it all feels so blissful:
This is when your body's feel-good chemical production is in
overdrive, and a biochemical wash of testosterone, dopamine,
and endorphins flow through it. Being in love can literally be
intoxicating, and certain endorphins work to increase energy,
elevate mood, and increase feelings of well-being. The same

endorphins are what increase sexual desire and make us feel so alive during this period.

This phase of enchantment involves plenty of laughter, playfulness, sexual energy, and excitement. Everything about the other person is interesting, and there is a desire to reveal as much as possible about yourself.

Most experts agree that this phase generally lasts anywhere from two months to two years and is the shortest lived of any of the stages of a committed relationship. The romantic stage is temporary, just long enough for the couple to connect and create strong bonds and appropriate commitments. It gives us a taste of the relationship's full potential but, unfortunately, it is a chemically induced taste and cannot last forever. The experience of "falling in love," however, should create a bond that helps the couple survive through the more tumultuous phases ahead.

People who are constantly hopping from one partner to the next may be trying to sustain this fantasy period, not wishing to progress to deeper levels of commitment. If you wish to succeed as a couple, be sure to hang onto these positive feelings so you can survive the next stage.

The power struggle begins

Sooner or later, idealized lovers become ordinary human beings. With the reappearance of this reality, a restlessness born from not enough separation and alone time becomes apparent. It is now time for both partners to return to their individual concerns in life.

Consider this the reality check. Your biochemistry has returned to its normal state, so you are able to see your partner's shortcomings. This is the period when a couple begin to deal with their obvious differences as the euphoria wears off, sometimes creating a time of disillusionment and conflict.

Here is where the real work of a relationship begins. The couple may begin to have more minor arguments that can escalate, or partners may become more withdrawn and isolated. Yelling may appear, often with shaming and blaming close behind. This early conflict is healthy and perhaps even necessary as both parties are instinctively jockeying for position in the new status quo, thus helping each partner separate a bit from the overconnectedness of courtship.

Feelings of ambivalence towards the other person may emerge, and each may wonder if he or she is still "in love." Both partners want the other person to change while they themselves remain the same. There is a fear of loss of control, and also a fear about the loss of interest in the partner.

This is when couples must learn the skills to be able to solve problems, listen to each other, and negotiate and resolve conflict. The main goal is to build trust. Many couples never move beyond this stage, and many divorces occur at this point. Couples who successfully handle this impasse do so usually through a renegotiation of the amount and condition of time spent together.

Reevaluation and separate identity formation

This stage begins with a fork in the road, when each partner begins to evaluate whether he or she wants to remain in the relationship. Reflection and reevaluation may tend to turn inward, with more isolation and distance between partners. People may disengage or emotionally withdraw. There may be feelings of disappointment. Sexual intimacy may become sporadic or nonexistent. You may miss the powerful emotions of courtship, and this is the stage when an affair is most likely to occur.

Partners may create a "parallel" marriage at this point, where activities, children, and hobbies take over the attention paid to the relationship. Children can be hard on a relationship at this stage.

There is a danger of entering a relationship "dead zone" at this point, where a person becomes bored with the partner and with life in general. A partner may bury him or herself in work or a hobby. The feeling of connection is greatly diminished.

For a couple to survive beyond this stage, communication, love, and trust are critical.

Awareness and transformation

If the relationship has survived until this point, there will be an interest in reconnecting. Both partners must realize their own fear of intimacy and how present behavior is shaped and influenced by what they learned and experienced as children in their family of origin.

They begin to see their own projections and distortions upon the other person. The war is over, and there is a desire to begin the work needed to build peace and understanding. There is a desire and willingness to learn how to work through conflicts and issues to achieve a satisfying resolution. It is a time to establish healthy boundaries, in which the couple can maintain separateness and connectedness.

The couple recognize that the relationship has the potential to be more than it is and that each has the power to make changes. They are willing to gain new insights about themselves, their partners, and their relationship, even if these are painful, in order to address the root of recurring problems. There is an acceptance of differences in a relationship.

Full acceptance

Research suggests that fewer than five percent of couples make it to this final stage. Each person is able to take responsibility for his or her needs and also support the other person. There is a great deal of warmth and mutual respect and a balance between autonomy and union. The couple has figured out how to resolve conflicts quickly. They work together as a team, and resentments are few. Each has chosen to be with the partner, flaws and all. This is often referred to as realistic love.

How does love change as we age?

Young lovers seek perfection. Old lovers learn the art of sewing shreds together, and seeing beauty in a multiplicity of patches.

~From the movie "How to Make an American Quilt"

This is the wisdom we gather as we age, much like the gathering of patches of cloth we enjoy, some of which remind us of important times in our lives. This is what I realized when I met Mike at age 49. My idea of love had changed dramatically.

Love had become less a seeking towards a perfect union, and more a gathering of all I had learned. Now Mike and I piece together our lives day by day into a quilt of varying shades and hues. It changes all the time, but it is always a thing of beauty!

Funny how, especially in youth, we think we will attract the most beautiful, together mates when we ourselves are completely messed up. We have low self-esteem and self-respect, and so we treat others badly; we simply haven't gained the level of maturity that makes us good company. But we still think a miracle will happen and the nicest, kindest, most together people will choose to spend their lives with us.

The other mistake we make with young love is we judge the book by the cover almost completely. The way our lover looks is so much more important because we want to make others jealous. Only later do we learn that jerks are jerks no matter how they look.

Expecting kids in their 20s to do love well is like expecting students untrained in math to ace their SATs. It just isn't going to happen! We all have to stumble around making difficult, painful mistakes until we mature and learn to know ourselves better. When we lose the tough outside armoring and get to know ourselves well, finally becoming loving and honest about our own flaws, true love becomes much more possible.

That is why I found midlife love so refreshing. When I met Mike I quickly saw that there would be no more nonsense in this relationship. We each knew far too well our own flaws and had acknowledged our deep need to be close with another who could accept us exactly the way we were. We had spent most of our adult years alone and consciously chose to take the risk and make the gigantic effort to welcome another trusting soul into our lives.

This relationship has developed into so much more than I expected at the beginning. I'm so glad I fought all the necessary battles within myself to get to this point in life. The reward is well worth all the times I searched for love and could not find it.

How is midlife love different?

I believe that our attitudes and romantic needs change in midlife and that the purpose of love changes throughout life.

Historically, the sole purpose of romantic love has been the continuation of our species. Without the attachment of romantic love, we would live in an entirely different society that would more closely resemble the social organization of the animal world.

The chemicals that race through our brains when we're in love serve several purposes, but the primary one is to make us form families and have children.

Once we have children, the chemicals change to encourage us to stay together to raise and protect the children. Cultural differences worldwide control how love is defined and displayed, but the fact that love exists in every human culture in the world is indisputable.

There are a few key factors that make us fall in love with a particular person. Research into attraction factors suggests that buried deep within our subconscious is a template for the ideal partner.

Appearance Research shows that we tend to be most attracted to those who remind us of our parents and even of ourselves. When shown digitized, morphed photos of their own faces, subjects always preferred these over other people's faces!

Personality Like appearance, studies show that we tend to prefer those who remind us of our parents in terms of personality, sense of humor, likes and dislikes, and various other attitude factors.

Pheromones The purpose of pheromones in the animal kingdom is to help us identify potential mates with an immune system different enough to ensure healthy offspring. Apparently, chemicals in human sweat also play an important role in love. When given males' sweaty T-shirts and asked to identify the one they felt most attracted to, the majority of females chose the shirts of males whose immune systems were the most different from their own.

Midlife love

The person who says it cannot be done, should not
interrupt the person doing it.   ~Chinese proverb

Obviously, when we are young and fertile, biological and
cultural factors play the largest role in determining whom we
are attracted to, and whom we decide to create families with.
How does that change with aging?

As we age, the power of biological and cultural factors re-
cedes, and our conscious brains step in to ameliorate the pow-
ers of our reptilian brain.

In other words, we know whom we are initially attracted
to, but then we begin asking more in-depth questions, like:
*Does this person show self-respect and respect for others? Is this
person good with money? Is he dependable? Is she loyal? Does
he have a good record of keeping commitments?* The more our
trust has been betrayed by previous relationships, the more we
insist on finding satisfying answers to these questions.

Over a lifetime, we hope to accumulate a healthy sense of
self-love and self-respect, which can act as our guiding light as
we attempt to find positive companionship in our later years.

And that's what's different about midlife. We no longer
seek the ideal partner to create children with. We instead seek
loving, positive, compatible companionship.

Would you want to marry in midlife?

If you are good at working out your differences, you share common interests, and your partner fills your needs and not just
your wants, perhaps you should consider making this relationship more permanent. If you desire the same kind of lifestyle

in your future, and you make each other feel special in the long term, marriage may be a good choice for you.

Midlife marriage: Learning to love our differences

How is marriage different in midlife? Do we ever begin to appreciate and enjoy the differences between ourselves and others? Or do we simply judge everyone else as wrong if they don't do things our way? Is love even possible in the middle of life? Or do we become too set in our ways?

I've personally experienced two midlife marriages. The first one, in my late 30s, did not succeed because we couldn't get over how different we were from each other. I would say the theme of our first year together was: *"I can't believe you do that, that way!"* We picked at each other so much that the center could not hold. In the end, there was little loyalty or love beneath all the judgment.

My second marriage, at age 50, has been much more satisfying and successful. Why? I would say because we are a much better match in terms of temperament, and more tolerant of the differences between us.

I'm sure this is true partially because both of us have spent most of our adult lives alone. We have taken on many challenges and long periods of extreme loneliness, and so we can more easily appreciate the positive impact the presence of another loving soul can have on our lives. We both know from personal experience that living alone is not ideal for either one of us.

We also have learned the value of giving each other lots of distance at times, and strive to appreciate the differences as well as the similarities between us. We consciously provide appropriate levels of solitude to each other as a gift. We are now custodians of our own solitude.

If one of us is unhappy or depressed, we give each other the privacy and space to deal with our own feelings. We know we do not have the power to fix the other's unhappiness, and know each of us will let the other know when we are ready to rejoin the human race with an improved attitude about love and life. We each take full responsibility for our own feelings and don't blame the other for various periods of unhappiness.

I have learned only recently to be aware that when I'm feeling critical of Mike, the personality characteristics that attracted me to him in the first place—traits like taking full responsibility and being detail oriented—can also get on my nerves: he can seem *too* careful or conscientious. At times like this I try to calm down and appreciate the dependable, responsible, sensitive, loving man I married.

Have your beliefs about love changed?

How have your beliefs about love changed by reading this book and processing where you've come from and where you are now? Have you found a way to get past some of your previous betrayals and found a new faith in yourself and what you deserve now?

Let's see what you now believe about love. Put an X next to all statements that describe your feelings most of the time:

_____ Finding an appropriate love partner is now a high priority for me.

_____ Sharing love is the most meaningful experience in life.

_____ I believe I am worthy of unconditional love and compassion.

_____ I love and accept myself exactly the way I am.

_____ I have a circle of family and friends who love and appreciate me exactly the way I am.

_____ I let go of relationships if they make me feel used or if they drag me down or damage me.

_____ I clear up misunderstandings with others as soon as they occur.

_____ I feel loving others teaches me much about myself.

_____ Feeling loved and appreciated makes me feel good about myself.

_____ A loving relationship is a safe and healthy place to get my needs met.

_____ I believe we are all loveable in some way.

_____ I believe I deserve to be loved for exactly who I am.

____ I believe I have the right to ask for what I want and need in relationships.

____ I say no to anyone at any time if I feel taken advantage of or abused.

____ I accept that some people will not like me. I can bear their lack of approval.

____ A relationship means that my partner will listen to and honor what I have to say.

____ I quickly sense when I am around toxic people and leave immediately.

____ Being in love renews my energy, making me feel like I can do anything.

____ I believe I will find the kind of love I seek if I approach it with an open heart.

____ I believe there are many others just like me, seeking the love they need.

Congratulations! You are changing and growing, and well on your way to believing in all that love can offer you in your journey towards wholeness.

Ask for exactly what you want this time!

And my heart came back alive. ~James Taylor

Now it's time to stop compromising and go out and get what you want and deserve! You have dealt with your past, feeling its full emotional impact, and so you are now ready to move on, stronger and more resilient than ever, free of fear and full of courage because you know who you are and appreciate yourself on a daily basis. You have much newfound trust in yourself and how much you have to offer others in relationships. And you finally *believe* in love again!

Will you find the strength and power within to ask for exactly what you want this time? Stop minimizing your hopes and dreams and make them come true! Do you deserve to be loved, honored and treated with the utmost respect? YES! Because that is exactly the way you treat others. You've learned how to listen to your own inner wisdom and to trust your gut, so you now know when others are treating you right, and have lost all tolerance for disrespectful behavior towards yourself or your loved ones.

This is what self-love feels like. Now that you have so much self-respect, you will begin to attract others who also feel great about themselves and their lives. Trust in the universe—true love is on its way to you right now!

Bibliography

Beattie, Melody. 1992. *Codependent no more: How to stop controlling others and start caring for yourself.* Center City, MN: Hazelden.

Brizendine, Louann. 2006. *The female brain.* New York: Broadway Books.

Browning, Dominique. 2002. *Around the house and in the garden: A memoir of heartbreak, healing, and home improvement.* New York: Scribner.

Buchholz, Ester Schaler. 1999. *The call of solitude: Alonetime in a world of attachment.* New York: Simon & Schuster.

Fisher, Helen. 2004. *Why we love: The nature and chemistry of romantic love.* New York: Henry Holt and Co.

Goldberg, Carl. 1990. *Understanding shame.* Northvale, NJ: Jason Aronson.

Kaufman, Gershen. 1989. *The psychology of shame: Theory and treatment of shame-based syndromes.* New York: Springer.

Lewis, Helen Block. 1971. *Shame and guilt in neurosis.* New York: International Universities Press.

Novak, Patti. 2008. *Get over yourself: How to get real, get serious, and get ready to find true love.* New York: Ballantine Books.

Paul, Annie Murphy. 2010. *Origins: How the nine months before birth shape the rest of our lives.* New York: Free Press.

Potter-Efron, Ronald and Patricia. 1989. *Letting go of shame: Understanding how shame affects your life.* San Francisco: Harper & Row.

Richo, David. 2010. *Daring to trust: Opening ourselves to real love and intimacy.* Boston: Shambhala.

———. 2002. *How to be an adult in relationships: The five keys to mindful loving.* Boston: Shambhala.

Romm, Sharon. 2004. *Dating after 50: Negotiating the minefields of midlife romance.* Sanger, CA: Quill Driver Books.

Salisbury, Anne. 2008. *Eureka! Understanding and using the power of your intuition.* Garden City, NY: Morgan James Pub.

Steinem, Gloria. 1991. *Revolution from within: A book of self-esteem.* Boston: Little, Brown.

Wegscheider-Cruse, Sharon. 1987. *Learning to love yourself: Finding your self-worth.* Florida: Health Communications.

Welton, Michele. 1999. *I closed my eyes: Revelations of a battered woman.* Center City, MN: Hazelden.